ENVISIONING ECOTOPIA

ENVISIONING ECOTOPIA

*The U.S. Green Movement
and the Politics of
Radical Social Change*

Kenn Kassman

Westport, Connecticut
London

Library of Congress Cataloging-in-Publication Data

Kassman, Kenn.
    Envisioning ecotopia : the U.S. Green Movement and the politics of
radical social change / Kenn Kassman.
        p.   cm.
    Includes bibliographical references and index.
    ISBN 0–275–95784–5 (alk. paper)
    1. Green movement—United States. 2. Social movements—United
States. I. Title.
    JA75.8.K37   1997
    303.48′4—dc20   96–44679

British Library Cataloguing in Publication Data is available.

Library of Congress Catalog Card Number: 96–44679
ISBN: 0–275–95784–5

First published in 1997

Praeger Publishers, 88 Post Road West, Westport, CT 06881
An imprint of Greenwood Publishing Group, Inc.

Printed in the United States of America

The paper used in this book complies with the
Permanent Paper Standard issued by the National
Information Standards Organization (Z39.48–1984).

10 9 8 7 6 5 4 3 2 1

Contents

Tables

Preface

The study of Green politics in America is a field that is rich and varied, yet one that has not been adequately explored. This is not to say that there have not been numerous valuable examples of research related to Green roots, both intellectual and organizational, or to Green values. The point is that this research has barely scratched the surface of its potential. The field of Green political thought and action still offers vast areas of academically unexploited territory. The purpose of this book is to raise questions as well as to provide answers. And I hope to spark new research in the field.

As a political scientist whose career has often entailed the study of the negative, I am sensitive to the concerns raised by the Green critique of the modern world. Given the abundance of evidence supporting the reality of Green issues (environmental degradation, violence, alienation, and social inequality— see table 1 in appendix A for a full summary), a starting point for this study was the acceptance that the Green critique of modernity has a legitimate base and is deserving of serious examination.

A second factor of importance in my undertaking of this project is the belief that the Green movement has the potential to become a significant political and cultural force. When considering the near future, Green thinking has several strengths. For the long-term future, a Green-oriented way of life may be even more necessary. Green ideology posits that modern society follows cosmologies, ideologies, praxis orientations, and visions of the future that perpetuate environmental and social dysfunctionality. The Greens do not stop at this critique; they attempt to positively alter these orientations. Greens search for alternatives and attempt to put those alternatives into practice. This combination of radical critique coupled with an active orientation toward social and cultural change could make the Greens one of the most important political actors of the next century.

The long-term significance of Green cosmology is perhaps the Greens' greatest asset. The ultimate importance of the Greens lies not in their rapid formation as a new social movement or in the current political successes and failures of the various Green political parties worldwide. Rather, agreeing with Bramwell (1989), Dobson (1990), Galtung (1986), and numerous others, I find that the potential for a long-term shift in civilizational consciousness lies in the cosmological orientation of the Greens. It is this possibility—that alternative Green versions of reality (when coupled with elements from the dominant worldview) are leading to the new cosmological underpinnings of the future—that I find most interesting (and heartening) of all. As a young father and believer in positive future possibilities, I hope that this book encourages further steps in this direction.

Kenn Kassman, Ph.D.

Acknowledgments

To personally list all the people who have offered me encouragement and helped me on my journey to this point in life would undoubtedly fill more pages than my editor would allow. So to my family, friends, teachers, and colleagues—you know who you are and what you've done—I appreciate it all.

Three people involved in this project do deserve special mention. My son, Kristofer, for whom this book was written. I hope your generation finds the courage to face the future in a positive way and the inner strength do the things that must be done. My wife, Birgit, who has provided more than I can say. And Dr. Glenn Paige, professor of peace studies at the University of Hawaii. Glenn was a constant source of inspiration and is a true bodhisattva in every sense of the word. This book would not exist today if not for these three people and all the others who have touched my life.

Finally, I want to say that this book is proof that the totally unexpected can happen. Don't be afraid to dream, and never let anyone tell you it can't be done.

The Green Phenomenon   *1*

Long before the Western concept of progress came into existence, there were
those members of the human species who envisioned better futures for themselves and their kind. Visionaries, such as these, be they the shamans, innova-
tors, and leaders of those earlier ages or the utopian dreamers, cutting-edge
scientists, and forward-thinking politicians of our own age, have shaped the
way their contemporaries have viewed both their external and inner worlds.
Visionaries transcend the day-to-day banalities of life to actively try to shape
the long-term future of their cultures and civilizations.

The United States of America has a long history of idealism. The early
colonists were people who sought a new and better life. Frustrated by the chains
that bound them to the Old World, these firebrands cast off their old ways and
created a new country based on the ideals of equality, liberty, and the pursuit of
happiness. Though a people may agree on societal ideals, clashing interpretations of goals and incompatible strategies for achieving aims often arise. In the
United States, basic conflicts arose at our nation's birth. The vastly different
images of preferable futures put forth by the Federalists and the Anti-
Federalists foreshadowed a struggle that has continued to this day. The stakes
in this struggle are high—nothing less than the shaping of public policy and
culture for the future.

Today, the Greens are one of the primary forces seeking to influence the
creation of America's future. They follow the long lineage of those Americans
who have struggled to expand social justice, democracy, nonviolence, and ecological harmony. But like America's Federalist and Anti-Federalist forerunners, the Greens find that similar value goals do not necessarily translate into
similar visions of preferable societies. This book looks behind the scenes of the
American Green phenomenon in order to analyze the similarities and differences its subcultures embody. The harmony and disharmony between the three

major Green subcultures is explored in detail. The eutopian and dystopian aspects of the subcultures are illuminated, and the potential impact of the Greens on possible U.S. futures is postulated.

The remainder of this chapter will place the American Green movement in a historical and global context. The roots of the American Green movement will be discussed first. The general field of Green political thought will then be introduced, and the argument that the Greens represent a new ideological perspective, with the power to threaten the currently dominant ideological systems of the West, will be explored. The organization of Green ideology into political parties and social movements worldwide will be examined next. Chapter 1 concludes with a discussion of the major historical, cultural, and psychological theories concerning the origins of the Greens as a global phenomenon.

THE ROOTS OF GREEN THOUGHT IN THE UNITED STATES

Brian Tokar (1987, 34-51) traces the roots of the Green movement in America to the social and political movements of the 1960s. Tokar contends that the civil rights, peace, and student movements were the first signs of an emerging new consciousness, with the feminist and environmental movements soon adding necessary input. By 1966 or 1967, Tokar argues, a genuine counterculture had been born. This counterculture rejected materialism, obedience to authority, and traditional work and sexual roles. As a liberated alternative to the dominant culture, values very similar to those of the Greens (living simply in harmony with one's environment, personal choice and freedom, nonviolence, and a communitarian caring for others) were evident.

Although Tokar concentrates on the 1960s as the genesis of modern Green consciousness, America has a long and rich history of thought that has contributed to the contemporary manifestation of these values.[1] This history is older than the United States itself, and though it has suffered many setbacks, being stronger in some times and places and weaker in others, American movements for positive social change have left a heritage that Greens would be wise to exploit. Personal freedom and social justice were advanced by early colonists in Rhode Island, Maryland, New Jersey, and Pennsylvania by their refusal to follow the European practice establishing official state religions. And though the situation was later changed by more oppressive policies, the first colonists in Georgia forbade the importation of slaves (Eggelston 1888). In Pennsylvania, nonviolence was stressed and military service was not required. Many early Pennsylvanians, being members of the Society of Friends, were opposed to warfare of any kind. Virginia and North Carolina also exempted their citizens from military conscription, provided they could produce a certificate of membership from a recognized peace church (Cooney and Michalowski 1987, 18).

Seeking self-government and freedom from oppression, early colonists formed the Committees of Correspondence as a nonviolent network organized to express their grievances (Resenbrink 1992, 28). Perhaps no individual of this time period more greatly personifies Green idealism than Thomas Jefferson, whose Anti-Federalist vision of America was one in which small farmers and small businessmen would govern themselves in a land where all men were created equal. Although bound by the conventions of his day, many of Jefferson's words still ring true today.

Movements for the expansion of democracy and social justice have always been present in American history. Opponents of slavery were able to abolish its establishment in territory north of the Ohio River with the Ordinance of 1787. By 1808 abolitionists had outlawed the importation of slaves into the United States. By 1820 all states north of the southern border of Pennsylvania had freed their slaves. Although it would take a bloody civil war to end slavery in the rest of the United States, these brave early abolitionists, the courageous women and men who worked the Underground Railroad, and modern civil rights activists offer many examples for the Greens to emulate.

The struggle for women's rights in America is equally inspiring. Although the society envisioned by today's ecofeminists is still only a dream, the long journey from a past described as "civil death" by Eleanor Flexner (1974, 7) provides evidence of the radical changes that can occur in society.[2] From Anne Hutchinson's challenge of the Puritan theocracy in Boston in the 1630s to the cutting-edge ecofeminism of women like Marti Kheel, one of the original founders of Feminists for Animal Rights, women have been major leaders in the fight for Green-related values. A striking example is Prudence Crandall, a Quaker who ran a school for "select and sheltered young misses" and opted to close her school in 1833 when the community protested her acceptance of a black girl. Crandall then promptly opened a school for black students and became a leading abolitionist (Flexner 1974, 38-40). Women like Crandall played major roles in every significant movement for social change in America. Frances Wright is typical in the kinds of wide-ranging activities that many of these women took on. Wright's fights for women's equality, worker's rights, the advancement of free education for all, and the Socialist Utopian movement of the early nineteenth century furthered several movements which have greatly contributed to the consciousness Greens exhibit today.

Ecological connection is another major root of modern Green consciousness. From the writings of early colonists such as Robert Beverly's *History and Present State of Virginia* (1705) to the environmentalism of Rachel Carson's *Silent Spring* (1962) to the poetry of contemporary Deep Ecologists, the natural environment as unspoiled by the trappings of man or civilization is presented as a paradisical utopia. Beverly equated the virgin purity of America with primitive ignorance of civilizational evils and put forth the idea of the free and noble Native American.[3] With this idea, Beverly began a long tradition of American pastoralism that persists in various forms to this day. Beverly's Native Americans are noble and free because they live in a noble, free, and very abundant Garden of Eden. Jefferson was later to adapt this argument into a political ideology, putting forth the American farmer as the backbone of democracy.[4] This ideological theme was translated into practical politics in the Homestead Act of 1862, which gave frontier settlers 160 acres of free soil (Smith 1950, 190-200). The democratic potential of the yeoman farmer became self-evident in the Populist revolts of the late 1800s, when those connected to the land rebelled against the exploitative practices of big business, big finance, and politics (Goodwyn 1976).

Movements such as transcendentalism followed the theme of nature as redemptive force. Thoreau's *Walden* (1854) is the classic text in this genre. Muir's writing in the early 1900s and Leopold's *Sand County Almanac* in 1949 are further major works adopting this theme. The advocates of wilderness (as opposed to agrarianism) as a liberating and restorative force were instrumental in the establishment of state parks (the first were Yosemite and the Mariposa Big Tree Grove, which were ceded to California by the federal government in 1864 with the condition they be preserved for the public), national parks (Yellowstone in 1872), and wilderness areas (in 1885 New York set aside 715,000 acres of the Adirondacks to be "forever kept as wild forest lands") (Allin 1982). This conservation movement was to change into an active environmentalism in the 1960s. The publication of Rachel Carson's *Silent Spring* (1962) woke the general public to the hidden dangers inherent in technological society and sparked a massive wave of reform that continues to this day.

Communalist, back-to-the-land, and utopian socialist movements have further contributed to modern Green consciousness. In the short history of the United States, several hundred of these communities have formed. Many of the early communes were organized around religious principles. These communities included the Shakers (1787-present), the Hutterian Brethren (1873-present), the Harmony Society (1804-1904), Oneida (1848-1881), Zoar (1817-1898), and Brook Farm (1841-1847). Later the utopian socialist communities such as New Harmony (1825-1827), North American Phalanx (1843-1856), Modern Times (1851-1866), and Utopia (1847-1851) were formed. Several of these communities greatly influenced larger society. Halcyon was the site of the first X-ray machine. New Harmony was the home of the first kindergarten as well as the first free public school system and the first trade school system in America. New Harmony also boasted the first free public library and first geological survey in the United States (McLaughlin and Davidson 1986, 86-87). Many of these societies encouraged nonmaterialism, nonviolence, social justice, ecological harmony, and democracy, and thus can be seen as significant forerunners of Green thought today.

GREEN IDEOLOGY

The values that the Greens seek to further are expressed in their ideology. Andrew Dobson, a primary theorist of Green ideology, has identified three main elements he views as necessary in any ideology: a description of the political and social world, a program for political change, and a vision of a preferable future.[5] Table 2, "Selected Summary of the American Green movement's National Program," in appendix A, illustrates the American Greens' fulfillment of Dobson's three criteria.[6] Analysis of several of the defined key policy areas in the Green program show critical descriptions of the social environment, visions of alternative Green eutopias, and active plans for alleviating identified problems of the present and moving toward more preferable futures. The Green program category concerning social justice, for instance, paints the picture of an overly materialistic, overly consumerist culture of the present that exploits and separates people into class, racial, gender, and sexual categories. The eutopian alternative offered by the Greens is a society where these categories no longer separate people. Strategies to achieve such a future include active incorporation of Greens into community-based struggles against exploitation and oppression, increasing one's education about one's own and other cultures, applying feminist perspectives throughout society, ending advertising that objectifies or manipulates, and support of sexual diversity.[7]

Green ideology poses a powerful challenge to status quo beliefs. In table 3, "The Green Worldview and the Dominant Worldview: Three Levels of Difference," in appendix A, I have summarized the critique of modernity and the proposed alternatives articulated by several of the major international Green theorists. One can see in the tripartite breakdown highlighting the perceptual, structural, and value differences between the Green worldview and the dominant worldview that a significant ideological gap exists between the two. The dominant worldview is seen by the Greens as aggressive and individualistic, stressing competition and domination over communitarianism and harmony. The result of these traits, say the Greens, is a limited view of the world that is leading toward a future of increasing personal insecurity and environmental degradation. Greens propose that a change must be made away from the anthropocentrism that views mankind as rightful exploiter of the earth and the social hierarchies that give certain groups more social rights than others. The general or composite Green eutopia is one where decisions are made at the local level, by those whom they affect, where disputes are solved in nonviolent ways, and where a communitarian mutualism exists between the human and nonhuman realm as well as in the social sphere.

Greens, in general, want to conserve the face-to-face relationships of the traditional polis and to expand the environmental pastoralism found in rural areas. They also wish to liberally expand social rights and tolerance of otherness. Thus their ideological place on the traditional political spectrum is not clearly defined. The majority of Green voters and supporters come from the

Left, but a number of them have come from the Right, as many as 24.7 percent in the 1989 election in Great Britain (Rudig and Franklin 1993, 42-43). Many early Green supporters were independent farmers displaying a rural bias, prejudice against large cities, and distrust of professional politicians. Other Green supporters, such as many antinuclear activists, are associated with the Left but display the same sort of populist distrust of large corporations and large government that is also expressed by segments of the Right. This mixture of constituencies and issue orientations has led some Green supporters to adopt the slogan, "The Greens are neither Right nor Left, but in front" (Capra and Spretnak, 1984, xxi).

Anna Bramwell believes that the strength of the Greens' conservatively oriented moral and cultural critiques coupled with the power of the critical reasoning and argumentation inherent in the Greens' use of the science of ecology has created an ideological force that has the power to directly challenge both liberalism and communism (Bramwell 1989, 4). The moral righteousness that many Greens feel certainly resembles the religious zealotry and patriotic nationalism found in many very effective movements today. As with fundamentalists of all varieties, some Greens feel their path is the one true way and are willing to go to extremes to express this.

The very presence of the Greens as an organized force must threaten the status quo. Dobson places the Greens in a position akin to that of the early liberals and the early socialists, who self-consciously called an entire worldview into question (Dobson 1990, 8). If Bramwell and Dobson are correct, then the Greens represent a force for change that could truly alter the way our descendants view reality.

There are many forces that shape our perceptions of the world around us. One of the most powerful, the mainstream media, has responded to the Green threat with attempts to delegitimize the Greens in the eyes of the public. The *Economist* ("Europe's Choice," 1983) has gone so far as to suggest that the Greens represent a "more insidious" danger to the stability of the German political system than the rise of neo-Nazism. The *New York Times* has repeatedly described German Green Party (Die Grunen) growth as "disruptive" and "unsettling" to old political alliances and describes the Greens themselves as "volatile." Kevin Carragee's analysis of *New York Times* coverage of the Greens concluded that "through varied framing devices the *Times* denigrated and depoliticized the Greens by characterizing Green Party members as lost children, quasi-religious zealots, idealists, and romantics" (Carragee 1991). John Ely notes that negative portrayal of the Greens in the dominant media is widespread and cites numerous examples, including an article in The *London Times Magazine* ("Waif at the Heart of a Revolution," 1983) that begins by comparing the nonviolent German Green leader Petra Kelly with Adolf Hitler.[8]

Antonio Gramsci's view (1971) that the dominant ruling classes seek to maintain hegemony of societal consensus (the meanings, values, and beliefs held by a population) explains these attempts to delegitimize the Greens

(Gramsci 1971). R. Williams (1977) contends that the hegemony of status quo elites must constantly be defended against challengers from outside. The status quo, seeking to maintain legitimacy, responds to the Greens by declaring them a threat. How this duel between competing ideologies will play out in the future is unknown, but it is likely that we are now witnessing its beginning rather than its end.

The contrary theoretical orientations, praxis strategies, and future visions of the Greens are major threats to the status quo, but they are also the movement's greatest source of strength. For those disillusioned by current ecological destruction, violence, alienation, and social injustice, a counterideological, antisystemic movement may seem to be a rational political alternative. Johan Galtung (1986) hints at this when he states that perhaps reliance on the old parties of the Right and the Left may itself be irrational, with the answers to modern problems existing outside of the customary way of thinking of traditional ideologies. According to Galtung's way of thinking, the Greens are not seen as a threat but as salvation.

THE INTERNATIONAL GREEN MOVEMENT

A further indication of the significance of the Green worldview can be found on the material level, where the impact of Green ideological formulations has manifested. Called by Sarah Parkin (1989) "the fastest growing political movement the world has ever seen," the Greens have become a global movement with organizations in over forty-seven countries.[9] Table 4, "Countries with Green Parties or Organized Green movements," in appendix A, illustrates the widespread appeal of Green ideology.

The New Zealand Values Party was the first national Green party in the world. Formed in 1972 by a political science student, Tony Brunt, the Values Party made an important impact not only on the way New Zealand voters but on the way the world looked at politics. The Values Party was successful because it put forth a cohesive set of quality of life and humanist positions underrepresented in the politics of modern industrial democracies (Rainbow 1993). Although the Values Party polled only 9 percent at their most successful national election in 1976, they sparked a worldwide movement for change.

In Europe, a variety of Green parties have successfully challenged the major parties in countries with parliamentary systems. Green representatives now serve in the parliaments of Austria (10 seats in the 1990 elections), Belgium (35 seats between two Green parties in 1991), Finland (4 seats in 1987), Greece, (1 seat 1990), Italy (33 between two Green parties 1992), Germany (8 seats in 1990), Ireland (1 seat in 1989), Luxembourg (4 seats between two parties in 1989), the Netherlands (6 seats in 1989), Portugal (2 seats in 1991), Sweden (20 seats in 1988), Switzerland (14 seats in 1991), and in the European Parliament (27 seats in the 1989 elections) (Feinstein 1992, 671-674;

O'Connor 1989). In addition, there are hundreds of elected Greens in local and regional offices in these countries and in Sweden (250 seats in local councils), Norway, the U.K., and France.[10]

Green activists in Lithuania, Latvia, Estonia, East Germany, and Hungary were important in leading the fight for their countries' freedom from domination by the former Soviet Union: Bulgaria now seats 10 Greens in its parliament (between two parties), Lithuania seats 8 (between two parties), Slovenia seats 14 (between two parties), and Latvia seats 7 (Feinstein 1992, 673).

Greens have organized in countries as varied as India, Japan, Australia, and Brazil. In the United States, over 80 Greens from thirteen states ran for political office in the 1992 elections; they received 560,000 votes and polled an average of 16 percent nationwide. Fifty-six Greens now hold elective office in fourteen states ("Greens Win 560,000 Votes in 1992, Seat 11 Candidates," n.d.). The Greens/Green Party USA (formerly known as the Green Committees of Correspondence), the largest Green network in America, boasts over 400 local affiliates.

Chandler and Siaroff see this political activity, especially in the electoral arena, as posing "a fundamental challenge to the established structure of political elites" (Chandler and Siaroff 1986, 303). Even in cases where Greens do not achieve direct electoral success, they are often seen as strongly determining the outcome of elections and governing coalitions. Muller-Rommel cites evidence that the German Green Party's activities encouraging ecological consciousness, nuclear policy awareness, and disarmament had a significant influence on public opinion as well as on policy decisions made by the major German political parties as early as 1985 (Muller-Rommel 1985, 484). Flynn and Lowe (1992) cite evidence that since 1988 "there has been a crescendo of interest" in Green issues in Great Britain, an example being the mainstream parties' formation of the Green Democrats and the Green Tory Initiative in order to compete for Green Party voters. A sign that the Green impact on the more traditional parties in Europe has not faded was in evidence at the February 1994 national convention of the present ruling party in Germany, the conservative Christian Democratic Union (CDU). The CDU decided on a vote of 359 to 277 to amend the term describing the party's fundamental socioeconomic policies from "social market economics," which it had used for the preceding 45 years, to the more modern and Green oriented "ecological and social market economics" ("Kohl Calls for Party Unity and Fighting Spirit," 1994, 1).

ORIGINS OF THE GREENS

There are four main theories that observers use to explain the rise of the Green movement on the world political scene. The first theory is utilized primarily by American theorists and posits the Greens as the political manifestation of a larger civilizational shift in consciousness. This theory of a New Age consciousness shift contends that a change in perception has swept (and is still sweeping) through the natural sciences and is now integrating its new interpretations of reality into the larger social arena. The second approach used in discussing the origins of the Greens has concentrated upon European manifestations of the Green movement and utilizes a sociopsychological theory of social change. This theoretical orientation involves viewing the Greens through the filter of their social backgrounds and individual value orientations to discover if a new post-materialist class has been created. The third theoretical approach is primarily European in origin and focus and concentrates upon the development of new social movements. New social movements seek major systemic and cultural change, separating them from more traditional social movements, which are viewed as primarily seekers of economic gain. The fourth theoretical perspective is one put forth by every subculture in the American Green movement. This theory sees the Greens as the modern manifestation of a dissident subculture or minority tradition that has existed throughout human history.

Paradigm Shifts and Social Change

According to New Age political theorists, the rise of the Greens can be attributed to a civilizational shift in human consciousness. Many New Age theorists believe this shift is similar to the theory of paradigmatic change advocated by Thomas Kuhn. A paradigm, according to Kuhn, is a particular constellation of beliefs espoused by a given scientific community at a given time. From this constellation of beliefs, scientists develop a view of what the world is and how the world works (Kuhn 1962, 1-9). A cosmology can be viewed as a similar device for society as a whole. It is a way to make sense out of chaos, to limit our sensory perceptions, and to form a solid ground upon which to stand. Paradigms and cosmologies are important because they form the basic building blocks of our reality. As we go through life, we add evidence to support our culture's dominant paradigm and we suppress novel discoveries that contradict our formulated worldview. Brian Swimme illustrates this point when he argues that in the paradigmatic sense, "scientists are fundamentalists."[11] In the cosmological sense, most of the rest of us are fundamentalists as well. As Hazel Henderson has stated, "reality is what you pay attention to" (Henderson 1981, xiv). By paying attention only to that which supports our views concerning reality, we are not threatened. We feel secure. This is why the Greens are so troublesome for so many people. What the Greens are doing is trying to get people to pay attention to occurrences and realities that they now ignore, suppress, and even deny.

Since paradigms are at least in part arbitrary, novel findings often threaten the paradigm by exposing different versions of reality. Many of these new theories about reality can be suppressed, but some cannot, because they offer better explanations than the dominant paradigm. When science can no longer ignore the new hypotheses and accepts them as the dominant "truth," the basic paradigm shifts. Often these shifts entail not only a change in theories but a change in perception as well. New Age theory holds that in this way paradigm shifts make themselves part of the thinking of the larger culture. As science, the dominant truth creator in our society, changes its way of understanding reality, it also changes society's way of understanding the world. Using political terminology, one can say that this shift in worldview is akin to a cosmological revolution.

Many Green theorists believe we are now going through such a cosmological revolution.[12] Fritjof Capra has used his background as a physicist to argue that a perceptual change towards what might be called the "ecological worldview" has been evident since the beginning of this century. Capra posits that the shift that he believes is happening occurred first in the hard sciences, primarily physics. Capra argues that quantum research (Einstein's relativity theory, Bohr's notion of complementarity, and Heisenberg's uncertainty principle) has undermined Enlightenment-based, Newtonian-Cartesian physics. Capra sees a new physics emerging that offers a more "organic, holistic and ecological" view of the universe than the old physics did.[13]

According to Capra, the dominant culture refuses to let go of the old worldview and clings rigidly to outmoded conceptions of reality. New Age theory holds that these old concepts and the values attached to them are no longer relevant to the modern world, and perhaps are even dangerous. The Greens, seen as the political articulation of the new ecological worldview, are viewed as what Arnold Toynbee calls "a rising culture" (Toynbee 1972). According to this theory, the Green movement as the representative of a more true and rational way of viewing reality, will continue to expand its following and eventually will assume the role of dominant worldview.

The Sociopsychological Roots of the Greens

Sociopsychological studies relating to the class background and value orientations of the members of the Green movement have primarily focused on the (West) German Greens.[14] The pioneer in this field is Ronald Inglehart, who predicted in the early seventies that a "silent revolution" oriented around value change was occurring in modern Western democracies. Basing his work on Daniel Bell's theory of postindustrialization (Bell 1973), Inglehart theorized that the prolonged era of prosperity and affluence that typified the postwar generations and caused a growth in tertiary, service-based, white collar occupations encouraged a large segment of those generations to abandon materialist values (the search for security through the stockpiling of private possessions) and switch their orientation toward the postmaterialist values of inner growth, quality of life, and environmental concern (Inglehart 1977). Inglehart's work spurred a burst of research into the value shift hypothesis, with results largely confirming his thesis. Hildebrandt and Dalton's (1978) follow-up research has shown that about 10 percent of the West German population meets these newvalue criteria. This is approximately the same proportion of votes that the Greens receive in national elections.

Membership demographics of the German Green movement seem consistent with Inglehart's new-class arguments. Manuel Dittmers found that Green voters are primarily young with over 70 percent being under age 35 (Dittmers 1986). Chandler and Siaroff (1982) discovered similar findings, along with strong support occurring among teachers and civil servants. Thirty-two percent of all Green Bundestag members come from a teaching background, fourteen percent from public service and seven percent from journalism careers. Over 53 percent of Green deputies were found to have occupations related to education, social science, or communication (Chandler and Siaroff 1986). Chandler and Siaroff's research confirms that Green voters come primarily from middle- and upper-class, salaried households. Poguntke's study of the German Greens, *Alternative Politics—the German Green Party* (1993) confirms the earlier research of Dittmers, and Chandler and Siaroff, and concludes that 70.2 percent of current Green Party supporters fall into the postmaterialist classification. A further 25.7 percent display mixed postmaterialist and materialist orientations (Poguntke 1993, 58-60).

There is evidence that Green consciousness or new-class mentality exists in America. Recent polls of American attitudes toward the environment show that 78 percent of all Americans consider themselves environmentalists, more than the total of Democrats and Republicans combined. Eighty-six percent of all American households say they recycle, and seven out of ten report that they favor protecting the environment even at the risk of slowing economic growth. In a Gallup poll survey taken in April 1991, the question was asked, "Is drastic action needed to save the planet?" Fifty-seven percent favored immediate, drastic action. Those indicating that immediate, drastic action was necessary were predominantly female (61 percent of all females responding), 18 to 29 years old (60 percent of those responding, with 30 to 49 years old a close second with 58 percent), high school or college graduates (59 percent and 57 percent respectively), and liberal (62 percent of the Democrats and 64 percent of political independents). Those with middle-class incomes of $20,000 to $49,999 (62.5 percent) supported the question by 15 percent more than those making more money and 6 percent more than those making less money. Fifty-nine percent of black respondents were likely to stress immediate, drastic action, compared to 57 percent of white respondents (Hueber 1991).

A more specific poll of American new-class prospects, by one of the major supporters of the American Green movement, shows results similar to those uncovered in Germany. More than 3,000 readers of the news digest *Utne Reader* replied to the poll. *Utne Reader*'s editors found that 72 percent of their respondents fit into the SRI International's Values and Lifestyles typology (VALS) under the category of "societally conscious."[15] This compares to just 11 percent of the United States population as a whole. VALS categorizes the societally conscious as those who believe in social change, rebel against materialism, and question a life dedicated to the traditional work ethic. When asked what issues are extremely important, 87 percent of *Utne Reader* respondents said world peace, 82 percent said nuclear disarmament, 65 percent said ending world hunger, and 52 percent said improving race relationships. Over 50 percent have contributed money to environmental protection, and 49 percent to antinuclear causes. This differs greatly from the American public as a whole, whose VALS profile for the large majority (70 percent) emphasizes belonging (38 percent), emulating (10 percent), and achieving material or status goals (21 percent) (Ogilvy, Utne, and Edmondson 1987, 121).

As for new-class demographics, 80 percent of the *Utne Reader* respondents were college graduates, and 50 percent have attended graduate school. Most had professional or technical jobs in areas like accounting, art, computers, medicine, law, teaching, and writing. Nine percent held executive positions in management or administration. Sixty percent made more than $23,000 a year, and 46 percent made more than $30,000. Eighty percent were between ages 25 and 45 (Ogilvy, Utne, and Edmondson 1987). This profile is very similar to that of the postmaterialist class posited by Inglehart.

These surveys indicate a ready constituency for Green politics in the United States. Many young, highly educated, professional, and secular citizens seem drawn to Green values. This may have serious implications for the future. New-class members have a political impact far beyond that of their average cohorts. More than 83 percent of the *Utne Reader* respondents regularly vote, compared to less than half of the American electorate as a whole. Ninety-five percent say it is important to make a contribution to society (Ogilvy, Utne, and Edmondson 1987). As older generations pass the responsibilities of societal leadership on to younger generations (or as younger generations force the transfer of power), it is primarily the professional and highly educated who will assume leadership positions. As many Green-oriented individuals are a part of this leadership class, it is likely that a small, but significant percentage of the positions of societal responsibility will be filled by Green-oriented societally conscious individuals in the future.

New Social Movements

Speculation upon the political implications of a new postmaterialist class has resulted in the theory of new social movements.[16] According to Jurgen Habermas (1981, 1982), new social movements arise in order to protect a social and cultural lifeworld from intrusion and colonization by the economic and political-bureaucratic subsystems of modern civilization. Habermas believes that traditional social movements such as the worker's movement could be co-opted and rendered nonthreatening to the status quo through the reallocation of goods. This assimilation into the social system is made possible as traditional movements see the larger purpose of the system, the expansion of the industrial sector, as basically good. New social movements differ from the older movements by rejecting reformism and demanding major social and cultural change. Ynestra King (1990, 106), illustrates this attitude by asking, "Who would want a larger piece of a pie that is rotten and carcinogenic to begin with?"

Habermas's theory holds that since new social movements arise primarily around issues concerning quality of life, self-realization, political participation, and human rights rather than issues relating to economic distribution, conflict must necessarily occur between the instrumentally rationalized (utilitarian) cultures of the economic-administrative system (big business and big government) and the new social movements. This sets up a very dangerous situation for the future. If the subgroups of the economic-administrative system are stifled in their ability to respond to threats to their domains of power with material means, they most likely will be forced to rely upon the other element of their worldview: domination.

As the dominating subsystems increasingly repress and seek to block new social movements from legitimate political (change-oriented) activity, one can expect increasingly radical responses from new social movement members. David Foreman (1991) states that the reason he formed Earth First! as a response to the destruction of wilderness in the United States was because, as a traditional environmental lobbyist for several years, he saw the instrumentalist orientations of the economic-administrative system constantly thwart any legitimate attempt to limit its growth. Foreman's response was expansion of the arena of political discourse to include extralegal tactics such as monkey-wrenching—ecological sabotage.[17]

The *Utne Reader* survey of Green-oriented individuals described earlier suggests that new social movement members push against the boundaries of political discourse almost as often as they participate in traditional political activity. One third of *Utne Reader* respondents indicated they have organized a political protest. Sixteen percent have committed an act of civil disobedience while only 18 percent have worked for a political candidate or party (Ogilvy, Utne, and Edmondson 1987). This seems to indicate a desire to participate politically, but it also indicates alienation from the choices offered by the two major political parties.

The Minority Tradition

Several Green theorists, primarily Americans, trace the genealogy of Green cosmological orientations back to prehistory. Social Ecologist Murray Bookchin (1982a) marks the beginning of the species itself and the origin of mother love as a starting point for the nondominating, nurturing attitude that the Greens seek to promote. Mystical Ecofeminist Riane Eisler (1987) believes the Paleolithic period, which marks the beginning of Western culture about 25,000 years ago, offers evidence of a more socially just, nonviolent, participatory and ecologically harmonious worldview where matriarchal, goddess-worshipping societies valued both women and nature. Neo-Primitivist Paul Shepard (1973) argues that hunting-and-gathering tribes were the "true humans" and that the advent of agriculture started a slow, degenerative slide to the present.

Devall and Sessions (1985) believe these diverse perspectives can be classified as a "minority tradition" that has consistently surfaced in the history of culture. The distinctiveness of the minority tradition is illustrated in table 5, "The Minority Tradition versus the Dominant Worldview," in appendix A. Devall and Sessions view the dominant worldview (underlying both liberalism and communism) as supportive of centralization, bureaucracy, and control. The dominant worldview, according to Devall and Sessions, sees nature as resource or data. The minority worldview they favor seeks decentralization, democracy, and simplicity while living in a harmonious community of people, plants, animals, and nature as a whole.

Devall and Sessions believe that the minority tradition is essentially universal. They see evidence of this in Native American cultures; Eastern philosophy, including Taoism and some Buddhism; events such as the Paris Commune of 1871; and in various utopian communities found throughout American history. Other theorists using the idea of a minority tradition are abundant in Green literature. George Woodcock (1990) cites the nonviolent anarchism, anti-industrialism and mutual aid of William Godwin, Proudhon, Tolstoy, Gandhi, and Kropotkin as examples of the minority tradition. Ursula LeGuin (1989), Gwaganad (1989), and Marie Wilson (1989), give examples of this tradition in Native American cosmologies. Corinne Kumar D'Souza (1989), Anne Cameron (1989), and Pamela Philipose (1989) speak of the tradition in indigenous peoples worldwide. Kirkpatrick Sale (1990) believes the minority tradition manifests itself today in a variety of ways other than what people commonly think of as Green. Sale believes some subcultures of anarchism, witchcraft, communalism, feminism, and monkeywrenching exhibit or lead to minority-tradition consciousness (Sale 1990, ix-x).

SUMMARY

When examining the roots of Green consciousness in diverse cultures and time periods, it appears that an idealistic longing for a just, nonviolent, participatory, and ecologically healthy society is fairly universal. There are several major theories that posit that such a consciousness is increasingly emerging in modern industrial societies. The people who exhibit this consciousness may be those who could become societal leaders, yet they often seem alienated from traditional politics. Still, Green consciousness represents a threat to the dominant status quo as it demands major societal and cultural changes.

NOTES

1. Unfortunately, this is not the proper place to discuss in depth the rich history of social movements stressing Green-related values. This brief summary is merely meant to give the reader a feel for some of the major currents that have contributed to modern Green consciousness.

2. A past where women had no right to property or to legal existence outside their husband or father and no right to vote.

3. Robert Beverly, *The History and Present State of Virginia*, ed. Louis B. Wright (1705; reprint, Chapel Hill: University of North Carolina Press, 1947).

4. The difference between Beverly's untouched landscape and Jefferson's modified landscape can be seen throughout the history of ecophilosophy in America. In the modern American Green movement it is typified in the ideological split between the Deep and Social Ecologists.

5. Andrew Dobson, *Green Political Thought* (Boston: Unwin Hyman, 1990), offers a view of ideology more specific than the traditional political science definition. For example, Plamenatz describes ideology as "a set of closely related beliefs or ideas, or even attitudes characteristic of a group or a community" (John Plamenatz, *Ideology* [New York: Praeger, 1970, 15]). Roy Macridis, *Contemporary Political Ideologies* (New York: HarperCollins, 1992), an analysis of political ideologies, offers another perspective. According to Macridis's definition, the Greens have developed a counterideology rather than an ideology. This is due to the Green questioning of the status quo and their attempts to modify the dominant belief systems of society. In Macridis's view, ideologies seek to rationalize the status quo, while counterideologies challenge it.

6. *The Greens/Green Party USA Platform* document was created and formalized in a committee process that stressed consensus and stretched over several years and two national conventions. Over 200 policy statements were analyzed and synthesized by 300 participants from 40 states at the first conference in Eugene, Oregon. Comments were then solicited from people unable to attend the Eugene conference. These were incorporated into the final document, which was ratified by a similar gathering in Boulder, Colorado, in September 1990.

7. "SPAKA: Green Program USA," *Green Letter/Greener Times* (Autumn 1989), 11-15, and The *Greens/Green Party USA, Program* (Prompt Press: Camden, NJ, 1992).

8. For a detailed list of derogatory statements about the Greens in the mainstream media, see John Ely, "The Greens of West Germany" (paper presented at the Annual Convention of the American Political Science Association, August 28, 1986), footnote 11.

9. The "forty-seven countries" is from Mike Feinstein, *Sixteen Weeks with the European Greens* (San Pedro, CA: R & E Miles, 1992), and is illustrated in table 4. An article entitled "International Greens" in the *Green Party News* (September 1993, 3), put out by the Hawaii Green Party states that Green parties exist in sixty-seven countries, but gives no actual listing of which countries those might be.

10. These figures are from Feinstein (1992, 671-74): Mike Feinstein's *Sixteen Weeks with the European Greens* is a collection of platforms, interviews, and statements offering a good overview of the European Green movement.

11. Brian Swimme, "Paradigms and Paradigm Shifts" (*ReVision* 9, no. 1 [Summer/Fall 1986]: 20). This entire issue of *Revision* is devoted to discussion between

leading new paradigm thinkers. See *The Elmswood Newsletter* published by the Elmswood Institute (Berkeley, CA) for ongoing new paradigm discussions.

12. Fritjov Capra, "The Turning Point: Crisis and Transformation in Science and Society" (paper presented at the University of Hawaii Political Science Colloquium, Honolulu, 1986). Jay Ogilvy, Riane Eisler, and Charlene Spretnak express similar views in "Paradigms and Paradigm Shifts" (*ReVision* 9, no. 1, [Summer/Fall 1986]).

13. Dewitt and Graham concur, believing "no development of modern science has had a more profound impact on human thinking than the advent of quantum theory" (quoted in Nick Herbert, *Quantum Reality* [New York: Doubleday, 1985, 16]). According to Fritjov Capra, *The Turning Point* (New York: Bantam Books, 1983, 38-39), this new conception of the universe can correct "a profound cultural imbalance which lies at the very root of our current crisis." Capra maintains that this imbalance, which is inherent "in our thoughts and feelings, our values and attitudes, and our social and political structures," is the result of a scientific paradigm and a society that has consistently favored a rationality that is fragmented, discriminating, and associated with masculinity, expansiveness, demand, aggression, competition, and analysis. Quantum physicist David Finkelstein agrees, "Our classical ideas of logic are simply wrong in a basic practical way. The next step is to learn to think in the right way, to learn to think quantum-logically" (quoted in Herbert 1985, 21).

14. One popular reading of value change, Robert Reich, *The Greening of America* (New York: Bantam Books, 1970), foretold of a Green consciousness change in the United States, while Ernest Callenbach, *Ecotopia* (New York: Bantam Books, 1975) took such a change to its logical extreme, with parts of the Pacific Northwest leaving the United States to form an independent Green state.

15. The VALS typology was developed by Arnold Mitchell, who describes Americans as falling into three major categories—outer-directed, inner-directed, or need-driven. The need-driven are poor. Mitchell subdivides them into survivors and sustainers. The outer-oriented make up the majority and are belongers, emulators, and achievers. The inner-directed types make up 20 percent of the American population and include the I-am-me, experientials, and societally conscious subtypes. See Jay Ogilvy, Eric Utne and Brad Edmondson, "Boom with a View" (*Utne Reader*, no. 21 [May/June 1987]) for more background on the VALS typology.

16. See Paul D'Anieri and colleagues, "New Social Movements in Historical Perspective" (*Comparative Politics* 22, no. 4 [July 1990]); Robin Eckersley, "Devining Evolution" (*Environmental Ethics* 11, no. 2 [Summer 1989]); Klaus Elder, "A New Social Movement?" (*Telos*, no. 52 [Summer 1982]); Jurgen Habermas, "New Social Movements" (*Telos*, no. 49 [Fall 1981]); and Saral Sarkar, "The Green Movement in West Germany" (*Alternatives* [April 1986]), for an overview of new social movement theory in relationship to the Greens.

17. The ecodefensive actions of Earth First! fit into Anna Bramwell's theory (explored in *Ecology in the Twentieth Century* [New Haven: Yale University Press, 1989, 18]) that new social movements, like early Marxists, create new categories of political discourse by straining against the bounds of the ordinary, and thus they extend those boundaries.

The American Green Movement   2

The success of the European Greens as a political force encouraged Green-oriented individuals in the United States to advocate the formation of Green networks in America.[1] As early as 1983, there had been attempts to organize American Greens (Baranoff 1988). Nationally, these attempts have resulted in loose networks of local affiliates rather than a solid party or organized movement (Satin 1989, Resenbrink 1992). There are many reasons for this. Greens tend to organize around local rather than national issues (as per the Green slogan, "think globally, act locally"). The American majoritarian electoral system is also a factor. In many parliamentary systems a party only needs 5 percent of the total vote for parliamentary representation; in the majoritarian system a party needs 50 percent (plus one vote) for a two-party race or 33 percent (plus one vote) for a three-party race. The apolitical attitude of the American people as a whole must also be taken into account. In many other countries elections average 70 to 80 percent voter turnout, while national American elections are lucky to poll 50 percent of the eligible voters. Local elections in the United States usually poll even less. Finally, the Green cosmology itself disdains centralization and charismatic leadership.[2]

The most successful of the Green networks in America was formed in 1984 in St. Paul, Minnesota. Influenced by the Capra and Spretnak book *Green Politics* (1984), the group called itself the Committees of Correspondence (CoC) after the Revolutionary War network of the same name.[3] The CoC has since changed its name to The Greens/Green Party USA. According to Steve Chase, attendance at the first CoC gathering mirrored that of the early German Green Party (Die Grunen) membership, including "farmers and community leaders, peace advocates, activists in churches and synagogues, environmentalists, teachers and others" who came together to create "a movement for the far reaching moral, political and spiritual renewal of America" (Steve Chase, undated letter).

The Committees of Correspondence resembled Die Grunen in one other important way: They adopted the four pillars of the German Green movement (ecology, social justice, nonviolence and grassroots democracy) as their primary value orientations. The CoC later Americanized the four pillars by adding six additional elements (decentralization, community-based economics, postpatriarchal values, respect for diversity, global responsibility, and future focus) to form a statement they called the "Ten Key Values."

The four pillars of Die Grunen and the ten expanded values of the CoC have found resonance throughout America. By April 1987, the CoC had grown into a network of 65 locals. By August 1992 the CoC boasted a membership of over 425 local affiliates.[4] The growth in CoC membership, coupled with its early formation and longevity, makes the network one of the primary Green voices in America today. This should not be taken to mean that the CoC are unchallenged in their representation of American Green orientations. Since its inception, the network has been accused of elitism, orthodoxy, and censorship. Green political parties in several states have refused to join the CoC, preferring their independence.

Other challenges to the CoC have also appeared. Dana Beal and the Yippies have held rival national conferences and publish the independent and anarchist news journals *Green Action* and *Overthrow*. Beal's primary platform difference with the CoC concerns the legalization of marijuana (Yippies strongly support, the CoC takes no official position). Beal's primary strategic difference concerns Green networking with already established third parties (Yippies strongly support, the CoC is hesitant). The 1992 elections show why. When Green Party candidates ran against other third-party candidates, they averaged over twice as many votes as candidates for the Libertarian Party and 68 percent more votes than all other third parties and independents combined, ("Greens Win 560,000 Votes," N.D.). The CoC has further accused the Yippie Greens of being overly centralized and elitist, a charge the Yippies also levy against the CoC (Baranoff 1988; Hill and Hawkins 1988).

The Democratic Socialists of America have also taken an aggressive stand towards co-optation of the Green vote by establishing Red/Green caucuses within its organization and publishing the *Eco-Socialist Review* and the *DSA Green News*. *The Activist*, the journal of the Youth Section of the Democratic Socialists of America, has repeatedly emphasized the need for Green-Socialist linkage (Hughes 1989, O'Connor 1989). James O'Connor's journal *Capitalism, Nature and Socialism* stresses similar linkage, although from a much more Marxist than Green position. The CoC has steered clear from such coalitions so far. Many Greens view socialism in a suspicious light ("Role of Eco-Capitalism," 1989, 1 ff.) and others critique it as part of the same nature-exploiting worldview as capitalism (Porritt 1985).

Overall Green-related activity has increased in the last few years. New organizations outside the CoC network include a coalition calling itself The Green Movement, which has established a Washington DC headquarters to link activists from the farm movement, women's, and African-American groups. A political action committee called GreenVote with headquarters in Boston, has organized to support pro-choice/pro-environment initiatives and candidates, and The Green Politics Network has formed to promote the creation of state Green parties.[5] Independent Green parties have formed in several states. The Hawai'i Green Party has elected a councilperson at the county level. In the 1996 elections, Green parties throughout the country supported Ralph Nader as their presidential candidate.

Dissent within the CoC has also blossomed in recent years. A major group of CoC supporters has formed the Left Green Network, while another Social Ecologist-oriented subgroup has formed the Youth Greens. The Left Green Network and Youth Greens are highly critical of many CoC members, especially those oriented toward Mystical Deep Ecology and Neo-Primitivism (Biehl 1988; Bookchin 1988b; Chase 1991). Social Ecologists seek a more mainstream (for the Greens) and political approach that concentrates upon social justice as much as ecology. This is reflected in the Social Ecologist rewriting of the CoC ten key values to include "ecological humanism, social ecology, racial equality, social ecofeminism, gay and lesbian liberation, cooperative commonwealth, human rights, non-aligned internationalism, independent politics, direct action, radical municipalism, strategic nonviolence and democratic decentralism."[6]

Stating that they formed only because they wished to add diversity to the CoC, the Left Green Network and Youth Greens have sparked much debate about who is or who is not a "true" Green. Mystical Deep Ecologists and Neo-Primitivists have come under bitter attack by CoC Social Ecologist-oriented members. In return, the Social Ecologists are accused of playing power politics and attempting to take over the CoC without regard to the large constituencies that make up Green subcultures other than their own.[7]

This divisiveness seem to indicate a state of chaos and incoherence within the American Green movement. Despite its internal difficulties, the CoC has managed to maintain its legitimacy with most local Greens, ratify a national policy program, adopt a national action plan, and form a nationally focused political organization. In recent years, it has managed to double the number of its local affiliates. Benoit Mandelbrot's work in chaos theory may thus be appropriate here. Mandelbrot states that inherent in what seems to be chaos are patterns not yet understood.[8] Barbara Jancar's (1992) "Chaos as an Explanation of the Role of Environmental Groups in East European Politics" sees localized Green groups as fractuals of larger movement patterns typifying common responses to the ills of the modern world.

This book argues that both Mandelbrot's and Jancar's observations are correct and that the internal "chaos" that the American Green movement is experiencing is not chaos at all, but is a phenomenon to be expected, given the three separate and identifiable subcultures within the movement. These subcultures have vastly different worldviews, praxis orientations, and visions of preferred futures. As one follows the chapters of this study, the patterns of coherence in the seeming chaos surrounding the American Green movement become clear.

WORLDVIEW SIMILARITIES IN AMERICAN GREEN SUBCULTURES

All three subcultures of the American Greens share basic characteristics that English observers of the Greens have begun to label as "ecologistic" (Dobson 1990, Bramwell 1989). Andrew Dobson describes ecologism as an ideology that is based upon an understanding of ecological and ontological precepts and that desires to restructure the whole of modern political, social, and economic life. Bramwell's definition of ecologism agrees with Dobson's, and in addition, Bramwell has distinguished thirteen traits that she associates with ecologism:

1. The belief that modern rationality does not pay enough attention to intuition
2. The hunt for a scapegoat who "made" society go wrong
3. Belief in the essential harmony of nature
4. Responsibility for one's actions
5. Apocalyptical beliefs
6. The belief that ecologists are able to plan a better society
7. Appreciation of aesthetic values and sensuous pleasures
8. Hostility to the formal and the elaborate
9. A search for a one-to-one relationship between man and object
10. An underlying moral stance
11. Skepticism towards science but not rejection of science or objectivity
12. The rejection of the existing political system be it capitalist or socialist
13. Putting faith in one's individual judgment ahead of party allegiance (Bramwell 1989, 15-21).

Bramwell's thirteen traits of ecologism correspond well with certain stances of the American Greens, but they also leave out critical differences between ecologism and Green political thought. Bramwell agrees with this and admits that while all Greens are ecologists, not all ecologists are Greens.[9] Brian Tokar's work helps us distinguish between the two. Tokar states that at the core of Green thought is the call for radical political and economic democracy, a new understanding of humanity as one element in an intricate web of ecological relationships, a radical critique of social stratification and hierarchies of control and domination that lead to social injustice, and a strong orientation toward peace and nonviolence. Chapters 2 through 5 of this study examine just how well the three subcultures relate to this core and where they deviate.[10]

A final and very important similarity between the three subcultures occurs on the level of community design and large-scale political affiliation, where all three Green subcultures share the bioregional vision. Under the bioregional vision, the boundaries of the nation-state and its political subentities would be superseded by affiliation to one's immediate geographical area (Bramwell 1989, 226). Natural borders such as rivers, mountains, and ecosystems serve to distinguish these bioregions from one another. The bioregional vision places emphasis upon learning the ecological interactions of one's own place and living within those interactions to as large a degree as possible.[11]

WORLDVIEW DIFFERENCES BETWEEN MAJOR SUBCULTURES WITHIN THE AMERICAN GREEN MOVEMENT

The Neo-Primitivist Worldview

The major precepts of the Neo-Primitivist worldview can be stated as follows: (1) wilderness is a realm of ultimate freedom, (2) immersion in wilderness leads to the realization of biocentric egalitarianism, and (3) the worldview of modern civilization is destroying the biosphere. These precepts lead to a negative orientation toward modernity and a desire to return to earlier times, as early as the Paleolithic age, seen as full of ecological harmony and personal freedom.

In the Neo-Primitivist worldview, wilderness is glorified as an arena of freedom where escape from the domination and repression inherent in the modern world is possible. David Foreman (1991, 5) states his belief that humans ought to become wild because "wild animals cannot be ruled." Devall and Sessions take this argument even further by citing Henry David Thoreau's testimony to the positive effects of integration with the wild: "In wildness is the preservation of the world. . . . Life consists of wildness. The most alive is the wildest. Not yet subdued to man, its presence refreshes him. . . . In short, all good things are wild and free."[12]

The Neo-Primitivist views wilderness in such a way because they see modern civilization as attempting to control all forms of nature, internal and external. These attempts are not seen as positive, but as negative, and are cited as diminishing important aspects of human existence, including the needs for spontaneity, independence from technology, emotional freedom, and freedom from systematic authoritarian repression. As David Foreman states (1991, 4-5), "We must break out of society's freeze on our passions, we must become animals again. . . . Damn it, I am an animal. A living being of flesh and blood, storm and fury. The oceans of the Earth course through my veins, the winds of the sky fill my lungs, the very bedrock of the planet makes my bones. I am not some New Age android."

In the eyes of Neo-Primitivism, the only way to recover the passion Foreman advocates and eliminate the negativities associated with civilization and
modernity is to reject these forms of social structure completely. Peter Berg
(1990a, 29) maintains that only by using wilderness as a model can humanity
avoid the "enslavement" inherent in current society. Earth First! cofounder
David Foreman (Foreman and Haywood 1987, 17) goes even further, believing,
"We haven't had any progress on this planet in sixteen thousand years." Berg
(1990, 21), while not quite concurring with Foreman, does say that "to discover
our wildness, the wild homo sapiens being within us, is very liberating. . . . It is
the future from my point of view."

The Neo-Primitivist worldview posits that the freedom found in the rejection of civilization will give humanity a newfound (renewed) sense of self. Neo-
Primitivists argue that this new self is not the isolated, individualized self of
modern liberalism; instead, it is a self embedded in communitarian relationship
with one's environment. The new self of the Neo-Primitivist is based upon the
elimination of modern boundaries between self and environment, an elimination that the Neo-Primitivist believes will lead to less alienation and thus
greater self-fulfillment. Foreman (1991, 6) argues that it is only through direct
interaction with wilderness that one can experience the full connection between
mind, body, and the larger world that surrounds oneself.

In the Neo-Primitivist worldview, the negation of dualism through this
new sense of self leads to a new ethics that rejects human self-interest as the
sole measure of worth. David Foreman (1991, 53) argues that "the ecological
community is not just valuable for what it can provide human beings. Other
beings, both animal and plant, and even so-called 'inanimate' objects such as
rivers, mountains, and wilderness habitats are inherently valuable and live for
their own sake." Foreman's Neo-Primitivism thus sees wilderness or the state
of nature as an egalitarian realm of freedom in much the same sense as did
John Locke. Locke believed the state of nature was "a state of perfect freedom"
where the "law of Nature. . . teaches all mankind who will but consult it, that
. . . no one ought to harm another in his life, health, liberty or possessions. . . as
if we were made for one another's uses" (Locke [1690] 1972, 396). There are
major differences, of course, between Locke's seventeenth-century view of nature and the modern Neo-Primitivist worldview. Locke did not extend the state
of freedom, equality, and self-actualization to the nonhuman world. Neo-
Primitivism does exactly this through its recognition of agency in the nonhuman world as well as its conception of intrinsic worth. As John Dryzek (1990,
206) has stated, "Regardless of its source, any recognition of agency in nature
clearly undercuts the Cartesian subject-object dualism that legitimates the
domination of nature—just as a recognition of human agency undermines the
instrumental manipulation that legitimates authoritarian politics."[13]

Neo-Primitivism argues that what all this means is that "we have a moral
obligation to preserve wilderness and biodiversity, to develop a respectful and
symbiotic relationship with that portion of the biosphere which we do inhabit,

and to cause no unnecessary harm to non-human life" and that "these moral obligations frequently supersede the self-interests of humanity" (Foreman 1991, 116).

Neo-Primitivists can take such a radical position because they fear modern society not only represses human nature but also disrupts the basic life-supporting processes of the biosphere.[14] In the Neo-Primitivist view of the modern world, technological man has become a cancer that assimilates all it can and destroys that which it cannot make like itself. The result is that Neo-Primitivists see war as an apt metaphor to describe the relationship between modern humanity and the nonhuman environment.[15] This leads to a decidedly misanthropic perspective among many Neo-Primitivists and betrays the nonviolence stance of the larger Green movement. Leading Neo-Primitivists have stated that they agree with John Muir's statement that "if it ever came to a war between the races, he would side with the bears."[16]

Earth First!, the primary Neo-Primitivist network in America, is composed of members who believe the well-being of the earth must come first before that of any individual species, including the human species. One writer to the *Earth First! Journal*, a mother with two children, has stated, "If the Earth is lucky, maybe humans will kill themselves off completely within the next few decades" (Jacobs 1989, 3). Christopher Manes (1990b, 29), a leading Neo-Primitivist spokesperson believes that "there isn't one scrap of evidence that Homo Sapiens is superior or special or even more interesting than, say, lichen." Manes sees misanthropy not as a potential problem but as leading toward a "richer, nobler, humbler way of life." Another *Earth First! Journal* contributor, Sarah Bearup-Neal (1990, 30), apparently agrees; she has stated, "I am fonder of trees than I am of people."

The perspectives cited here are not the isolated views of a few alienated individuals. Earth First! was created by five environmental activists on April 4, 1980. It has since grown into an international movement with an estimated 50,000 adherents in North America, a published journal with 15,000 readers, and a network of activist cells that participate in aggressive political action oriented toward stopping wilderness destruction in all its forms. Although there are many smaller networks that represent the Neo-Primitivist worldview, Earth First! is the example that best typifies the Neo-Primitivist worldview.

The Worldview of Mystical Deep Ecology

The worldview of Mystical Deep Ecology is one that has existed as long as human beings have had conscious recognition of the world around themselves. Called the religious-metaphysical worldview by Jurgen Habermas (1984, 1987), this cosmological perspective sees an enchanted and immanent world full of communicative, interactive, self-actualizing beings who are inherently valuable in their own right.[17] Mystical Deep Ecology posits that modern ways of viewing the world lead to objectification of otherness and alienation of self; a situation

where Devall and Sessions (1985, 67 and 48) believe "we see ourselves as isolated and narrow competing egos" encompassed in a worldview that "has as its
ultimate vision the total conquest and domination of nature."

The worldview of Mystical Deep Ecology puts forth an alternative vision of
reality where a mystical, magical, enchanted world offers a sense of belonging
by positing the earth as a living body that has its own teleology. Paula Gunn
Allen (1990, 52) describes the planet earth as a body composed of many smaller
beings each having their own needs, aims, goals, and processes. Allen believes
that not only the earth is alive in this way, but all other planets are as well. Allen's view of life, like that of most Mystical Deep Ecologists, includes planetary
"by-products or expressions, such as animals, vegetables, minerals, climatic
and meteorological phenomena."[18] These smaller entities, or "byproducts and
expressions," are seen by the Mystical Deep Ecologist as comprising immanent
parts of a sacred totality. Luisah Teish (1985) summarizes this conception of
reality with an ancient African adage, "We are all cells in the body of God."

This axiological, teleological, and immanent view of nature leads Mystical
Deep Ecology to a biocentric egalitarianism that calls for restraint on human
instrumental activity. For Starhawk (1989, 177), the Mystical Deep Ecology
worldview "challenges our sense of values. . . . Each being has a value that is
inherent, that cannot be diminished, rated, or ranked, that does not have to be
earned or granted." In the Mystical Deep Ecology worldview, human beings
lose their place of significance in the world and are seen as "no more valuable
to the life of the universe than a field flowering in the color purple, than rivers
flowing, than a crab picking its way across the sand—and no less" (Christ
1990, 66).

The reenchantment of this biocentric community adds a further restraint on
human action through the addition of a sense of mystery to the world. As Carol
Christ (1990, 66) explains, "Knowledge that we are but a small part of life and
death is the essential religious insight. The essential religious response is to
rejoice and to weep, to sing and to dance, to tell stories and create rituals in
praise of an existence far more complicated, more intricate, more enduring than
we are." To the Mystical Deep Ecologist, the proper role of the human individual becomes one of celebration of nature rather than manipulation of nature.

A number of Mystical Deep Ecologists have taken their worldview in an
interesting direction. These theorists can be classified as Mystical Ecofeminists;
their view differs from the larger school of Deep Ecologist thought through
their radical critique of patriarchic society. In the Mystical Ecofeminist worldview, patriarchy bears the responsibility for virtually every modern social and
ecological ill. Charlene Spretnak (1986, 30-31) illustrates this emphasis by
exploring the linkages she sees between the patriarchic oppression of human
and nonhuman nature in the following passage: "Patriarchal culture. . . con-
notes not only injustice towards women but also the accompanying cultural
traits: love of hierarchical structure and competition, love of dominance-or-

submission modes of relating, alienation from Nature, suppression of empathy and other emotions, and haunting insecurity about all of those matters."

Central to the Mystical Ecofeminist critique is the idea that patriarchal culture sets up dualities that, as Marti Kheel explains (1985, 136), "see the world in terms of static polarities—'us and them,' 'subject and object,' 'superior and inferior,' 'mind and body,' 'animate and inanimate,' 'reason and emotion,' 'culture and Nature.'" According to Kheel, these dualities always have two characteristics in common. One half of the duality is always valued more than the other half, and "the more valued half is always seen as 'male' and the less valued half as 'female'." Kheel maintains the result of this patriarchal emphasis on dualism has been "the ruthless exploitation of women, animals, and all of nature."

The Mystical Ecofeminist solution to the problems that beset a modern world dominated by patriarchy is the return to a more feminized, earth goddess-worshipping, matriarchal society. This goal sets Mystical Ecofeminists apart from those who believe women can only achieve full human status by joining men in exploits that express opposition to the natural world. Mystical Ecofeminists reject this view and advocate the linkage between women and nature as a positive source of power.[19]

In setting their matriarchic goals for the future, Mystical Ecofeminism presents a further refinement of Mystical Deep Ecologist thought. The Mystical Ecofeminist critique of modern ills is centered around androcentrism (the perspective that favors the view of men only) rather than anthropocentrism, as seen in the larger Deep Ecology movement.[20] Mystical Ecofeminism thus presents, in a clearer way, the extremes to which the main arguments of the Mystical Deep Ecology worldview can be taken. Mystical Ecofeminism can be used as a distilled representative of the Mystical Deep Ecology worldview.

The Worldview of Social Ecology

The worldview of Social Ecology has been aptly described by Robin Eckersley (1988) as "communitarian anarchism rooted in an organismic philosophy of nature." Developed over the past 50 years largely by one man, Murray Bookchin, Social Ecology has evolved into a complex set of ideas, values, and beliefs quite different from the biocentric Neo-Primitivist and Mystical Deep Ecologist subcultures of the American Green movement.[21] As in the other two subcultures we have described in this chapter, the exploitation of the natural world is a significant theme in Social Ecologist literature. However it is not the major theme. Social Ecologists believe the solution to environmental degradation lies in the sociopolitical sphere. Social Ecology posits that a society that accepts hierarchy and values one human being over another will naturally lead to a consciousness of domination.

The Social Ecologist worldview thus strives to reject domination in all its forms. Like Mystical Ecofeminism, Social Ecology supports the elimination of patriarchy. The Social Ecologist worldview also includes in its analysis the rejection of racism, sexism, ageism, and the structural violence beget by such hierarchical cultural norms. Social Ecology disagrees adamantly with the enchanted aspects of Mystical Deep Ecology and supports the abolition of all concepts of religious hierarchy and superstitious thought. To the Social Ecologist, mysticism subverts its followers through self-subjugation to a superior goddess. Social Ecology further rejects Neo-Primitivism. In the view of the Social Ecologist, Neo-Primitivism subverts itself to the will of a superior natural world. Both the Mystical Deep Ecologist and Neo-Primitivist worldviews are seen by Social Ecology as establishing hierarchies of domination, with a superior will above that of humankind. To the Social Ecologist, this situation is simply a reversal of the present state of affairs where modern humanity dominates the natural environment to the point of exploitation (Bookchin 1989, 78).

The danger that Social Ecology sees inherent in its fellow Green subcultures lies in the Social Ecologist view that there is no firm dividing line between the social realm and the natural realm. Social Ecology posits that despite their rhetoric, other Green subcultures fall into the same dualistic trap they seek to avoid. The result is "a systematic unraveling of the interface between nature and mind."[22] For the Social Ecologist, a consciousness containing any form of hierarchy cannot exist only toward one part of reality; the consciousness necessarily permeates into all arenas of human interaction. Thus the worldviews of fellow Green subcultures are seen to be as misguided as is the modern worldview.[23]

The Social Ecologist worldview posits humankind as a "remarkably creative and social life-form that is organized to create a place for itself in the natural world, not only to adapt to the rest of nature" (Bookchin quoted in Chase 1991, 33). This sense of human place in the world offers a middleground alternative to the modern placement of humankind as an alienated conqueror of otherness or the mystified subject of nature seen by Deep Ecology. To the Social Ecologist, the view of humans as highly evolved beings in a continuum of consciousness, able to reflect upon and control their actions, implies responsibility and the duty to their surrounding environment. Janet Biehl (1991, 126) argues that this view of reality also demands the development of an ethics of service to both the natural and the social realms of human existence. To the Social Ecologist, this duty to serve implies that, at the very least, human beings acknowledge the integrity and subjectivity as living beings of other life forms and recognize that nature demands some kind of recompense for human instrumental activity (Bookchin 1982a, 303).

Bookchin (1982a, 45) sees a possible model for this way of interacting with the world in the cultures of the Wintu and Hopi Native Americans and in the expression of mother love. The Wintu people do not have a concept of ownership or possession. Rather, they live with their surroundings. The Wintu thus lives with but does not possess his bow and arrows, just as he lives with but does not possess his children. Social Ecologists thus seek to extend the sense of solidarity and respect they advocate in the human realm to the nonhuman and even the inanimate world.

Interdependence is more valued than independence in the worldview of Social Ecology, but variety and individuation are also prized. To the Social Ecologist, the ideal societal relationship is the loving, nurturing, symbiotic interaction a mother or father (sometimes) has with her or his child. By stressing cooperation, interdependence, and respect for difference rather than competition, self-interested individualism, and fear of otherness, Social Ecologists believe their view of reality can change the modern world.

SUMMARY

The American Green movement is often viewed as chaotic and unorganized. There are many reasons for this, but the most important reason has been overlooked by movement observers. Drawing from chaos theory, it becomes obvious that there are patterns in the apparent disorder. As one begins to understand the similarities within the movement, the patterns of difference become starker. It is these patterns of difference that distinguish the three subcultures of the U. S. Greens and help explain the seeming "chaos."

NOTES

1. Fritjov Capra and Charlene Spretnak (*Green Politics* [New York: E. P. Dutton, 1984, 193-229]) saw the possible forms the American Green movement could take as network, movement, caucus within traditional political parties (two forms), and independent party. They concluded that organization as a movement was the most likely to be successful in the United States.

2. See Brian Tokar, *The Green Alternative* (San Pedro, CA: R & E Miles, 1987, 137); Alan Isaak, *An Introduction to Politics* (Glenview, IL: Scott, Foresman, 1987, 238 and 251); Capra and Spretnak (1984, 202-3); and John Resenbrink, *The Greens and the Politics of Transformation* (San Pedro, CA: R & E Miles, 1992) for further discussions of Green localism and/or third-party constraints in the American political system.

3. Mystical Ecofeminist Charlene Spretnak was one of the primary organizers of the first meeting of the CoC. Social Ecologist Murray Bookchin, Ernest Callenbach, and Harry Boyte, author of *The Backyard Revolution* (Philadelphia: Temple University Press, 1980) also attended.

4. Open letter to the Greens from Dee Berry (1987). See also *Green Politics* 2, no. 2 (Summer 1992): 7. It should be noted that many of these members are non-dues-paying, and many others do not participate in network decision making at all.

5. See Phil Hill and Howard Hawkins, "Dana Beal's 'Mid-Atlantic Greens' Are Bad News, but Not Because They Smoke Too Much Dope" (*Green Synthesis*, no. 28 [1988]); Zvi Baranoff, "Glastnost for the American Greens" (*Green Action* 5, no. 3 [1988]); and Alston Chase (1987) for an overview of the Yippie Greens. See "Green

Voting Resources" (*Utne Reader*, no. 53 [September-October 1992]) for an overview of "Green" organizations existing independently of the Committees of Correspondence.

6. The Youth Greens later renamed themselves the Campus Green Network. The ten values of the Left Green Network were stated in an open letter from the Left Green Network dated August 13, 1988.

7. See *Green Synthesis* (numbers 31-33) for a good look at the Deep Ecology/Social Ecology debates. Also see Murray Bookchin's "Social Ecology Versus 'Deep Ecology'" (*Green Perspectives*, no. 4 and 5 [Summer 1987]) and Steve Chase's *Defending the Earth* (Boston: South End Press, 1991).

8. Benoit Mandelbrot, ("Chaos Theory," Paper presented at the World Futures Studies Federation XIII World Conference, Turku, Finland, August 23, 1993). Mandelbrot also stressed that chaos theory is a theory oriented toward the natural sciences and not the social sciences. I agree with Mandelbrot and use chaos theory here as an illustrative metaphor.

9. Anna Bramwell argues in *Ecology in the Twentieth Century* (New Haven: Yale University Press, 1989, 21) that while there were fascist ecologists, fascism did not and does not have a Green component.

10. See table 1, "The Four Horsemen of the Green Apocalypse," for similarities between the Green critique of modernity, and table 3, "The Green Worldview and the Dominant Worldview: Three Levels of Difference," in appendix A for an overview of Green worldview similarities on the perceptual, structural, and value levels.

11. William Cronon illustrates the bioregional lifestyle among early-contact Native Americans in New England in his fascinating book, *Changes in the Land* (New York: Hill and Wang, 1983). See also Christopher and Judith Plant, *Turtle Talk* (Philadelphia: New Society, 1990), Van Andruss, Christopher Plant, Judith Plant and Eleanor Wright, *Home! A Bioregional Reader* (Philadelphia: New Society, 1990), and the North American Bioregional Congress's *Proceedings* (Forestville, CA: Hart, 1987) for more on the bioregional perspective.

12. From Thoreau's essay "Walking" (1851) in Bill Devall and George Sessions, *Deep Ecology* (Salt Lake City: Peregrine Smith Books, 1985, 109).

13. This line of argumentation leads some Deep Ecologists to argue that biocentrism is actually an extension of Enlightenment thought rather than its rejection. See *The Dreaded Comparison: Human and Animal Slavery*, by Marjorie Spiegel (Philadelphia, PA: New Society Publishing, 1988).

14. Shepard argues that by removing humanity from "a sense of place and time in the context of all life" human society has created a situation where it is destroying all life including itself (Paul Shepard and David McKinnley, *The Subversive Science*, Boston: HoughtonMifflin, 1969, 8).

15. James Lovelock believes that environmentally, "We are in a similar position to that of Europe in 1938. In those days one knew a war was looming, but nobody had the slightest idea what to do about it. There were a few sensible people who prepared for war" (Lovelock in "Only Man's Presence Can Save the Earth," *Harper's Magazine*, April 1990).

16. Muir in David Foreman and Bill Haywood, eds., *Ecodefense* (Tuscon, AZ: Ned Ludd Books, 1987, 17).

17. Habermas takes a negative stance toward the religious-metaphysical worldview and calls it "confusion between nature and culture" in his *Theory of Communicative Action, Vol. 1* (Boston: Beacon Press, 1984).

18. See Paula Gunn Allen, "The Woman I Love Is a Planet, the Planet I Love Is a Tree" in *Reweaving the World*, ed. Diamond and Orenstein (San Francisco: Sierra Club Books, 1990). Allen doesn't say anything about planets lacking the majority of these "expressions." It would be interesting to see how she views the moon in this regard.

19. See Simone de Beauvoir, *The Second Sex* (New York: Vintage Books, 1974), Janet Biehl, *Rethinking Ecofeminist Politics* (Boston: South End Press, 1991), Marti Kheel, "Ecofeminism and Deep Ecology" (in *Reweaving the World*, ed. Diamond and Orenstein (San Francisco: Sierra Club Books, 1990); and Ynestra King, "The Ecology of Feminism and the Feminism of Ecology," (in *What Is Ecofeminism?*, ed. Gwyn Kirk (New York: Ecofeminist Resources, 1990a) for an overview of this argument.

20. Marti Kheel (1990) is especially adept at pointing out these differences. See also Jim Cheney, "Ecofeminism and Deep Ecology," (*Environmental Ethics* 9, no. 2, (Summer 1987) and Michael Zimmerman, "Deep Ecology and Ecofeminism" in Diamond and Orenstein (1990).

21. Since 1974 Murray Bookchin has had the help of his colleagues at the Institute for Social Ecology, which he founded in conjunction with Goddard College in New England, in the development of Social Ecology theory. The view of Social Ecology we take in this book is larger than Bookchin's philosophy, but one should in no way slight his contribution to the Social Ecologist worldview. See Bookchin's many contributions in the bibliography for the basic tenets of Social Ecologist thought.

It should be noted that although Bookchin's view of Social Ecology has drawn much from the leftist tradition, including its emphasis on rationalism, its anticapitalist rhetoric, elements of its technological critique, and the methodological tool of dialectics, most Social Ecologists are critical of the economic reductionism, reliance on the working class as revolutionary base, and concept of a domineering nature contained in Marxism. See Bookchin (1980, 1986a, 1986b, 1987c) as well as Biehl (1991) for the Social Ecologist critique of Marxism.

Many Social Ecologists also reject the anticapitalist rhetoric of Bookchin as too inflammatory. Likewise, while many Social Ecologists adopt the communalism and mutual aid of Proudhon and Kropotkin and pay homage to the anarchist-syndicalist tradition, many Social Ecologists believe such traditions can no longer explain and mobilize the forces of modern change (see Bookchin 1985a, 1985b).

22. Murray Bookchin (1982a) cites the main figures in Enlightenment empiricism (Descartes), liberalism (Locke), and philosophy (Kant) as being the philosophical forefathers of this unraveling, through their articulation of dualities between the modern body and the soul, the perceiving senses and the perceived world, as well as the mind and external reality.

23. See tables 1, 2, and 3 in appendix A for a summary of the Green critique of modern life.

Green Praxis   3

In her analysis of the international Green Movement, Anna Bramwell (1989, 9) stated, "When cultural criticisms are combined with political action, it is time to take the phenomenon seriously." This is the case with the Greens today. Members of all three Green subcultures participate in common and traditional social change activities, such as lobbying, protesting, and minor civil disobedience. Each subculture also has its own unique praxis orientations followed by subculture adherents. These praxis orientations are not only derived from the theories of social change posited in the primary texts of the three cosmological subcultures but also from the day-to-day practice of Green living. In this chapter, we examine the differing transition strategies adopted by the three subcultures of the American Green movement as they attempt to modify present society and move toward the creation of their preferred futures.[1] The differences between subculture praxis strategies, grounded in the cosmological critiques and worldviews explored in chapter 2, lead us to the pathways of future possibilities explored in chapters 4 and 5.

PRAXIS AND NEO-PRIMITIVISM

Active Ecological Resistance

The dominant description of the Neo-Primitivist is that of Green warrior.[2] This is because of the aggressive prowilderness theoretical and action orientations advocated by Neo-Primitivists. Neo-Primitivism believes humankind has declared war upon the world of wilderness. Green warriors view themselves as nature's main human allies, and have adopted slogans such as "Earth First!" and "No Compromise in Defense of Mother Earth." Neo-Primitivists call their praxis orientation a variety of names including ecotage and ecodefense. Critics prefer to call these praxis strategies ecoterrorism.

To clear a value-laden and muddied field of terminology, I prefer the term "active ecological resistance" to describe Neo-Primitivist praxis. Active ecological resistance contains three primary elements. First, active ecological resistance is active in the sense that the tactics used are aggressive and proactive.[3] Arne Naess (1988, 261-265), has identified the second element of active ecological resistance, an intense ecological orientation involving identification and a sense of immediate connection with the natural world. This ecologism, as Andrew Dobson has described it, can be contrasted with mainstream environmentalism, which maintains that ecological problems can be solved within the framework of the present worldview without calling that view into question.[4] The praxis orientation of environmentalism leans toward reformism, such as demands for better management of industrial processes, recycling, limitations on pollutants, and cars with better gas mileage. Ecologism, on the other hand, demands fundamental changes in present political, social, and cultural beliefs, values, and structures. Calls by environmentalists to modify automobile emission standards are met by cries from ecologists to eliminate the need for cars altogether. Neo-Primitivists are ecologists in the fundamental sense, believing that duty to the earth (meaning the realm of the wild and unmanaged) comes before duty to any economic, political, or social structure.

When this ecologistic sense of obligation to the natural world is coupled with the aggressive action orientation already described, the third element in active ecological resistance is often awakened: an awareness of the power of the dominant economic, philosophic, and political forces that Neo-Primitivism finds itself opposed to (Foreman 1991, 122-23 and 144-45). This awareness leads to an anarchistic orientation of political resistance pitting Neo-Primitivists against virtually every form of legitimate power in modern society. This does not mean the Neo-Primitivist does not use powers such as the court system and legislative lobbying to its advantage whenever possible. What it does mean is that if efforts to achieve success within the system fail, other efforts undertaken outside of the system are viewed as equally legitimate.

Neo-Primitivism and Direct Action

Observers of Neo-Primitivism discuss two main kinds of praxis strategies. These can be described as overt active ecological resistance and covert active ecological resistance.[5] The primary orientation of both overt and covert active ecological resistance is direct action. In overt active ecological resistance, this action takes the form of civil disobedience and includes activities such as blockading logging roads with one's body, chaining oneself to trees about to be cut, and public education and publicity events that often lead to arrest. Chris Manes believes the roots of Neo-Primitivist overt active ecological resistance rest in the experiences of the 1960s civil rights movement and its emphasis on personal ethics, integrity, and the "rightness" of the cause.[6]

In the type of overt actions just described, the goals are twofold: (1) the personal/spiritual goal of "bearing witness against injustice" and (2) the political goal of making known to public officials and the public at large the fact that ecological destruction is occurring and that there is active opposition to such destruction.

Overt active ecological resistance has had many successes. Lawsuits linked to endangered species acts have cost timber companies and other wilderness "developers" countless delays. Expenditures in legal fees and the employment of idle workers cost these companies millions of dollars each year. But overt active ecological resistance also carries a price. Because it is direct and open, its practitioners can be easily targeted for retaliation. Protesters are often threatened and harassed, and their vehicles and houses are broken into and vandalized. While often anonymous, sometimes this harassment is openly undertaken by public authorities beholden to powerful interests or opposed to civil disobedience. The very real threat of personal injury or even death by those opposed to overt active resistance is of grave concern.[7] Arrest for overt active ecological resistance is the norm, and retaliatory civil lawsuits against active ecological resisters have become common.[8] As a result, Neo-Primitivists who wish to avoid these consequences and who feel that even stronger measures must be taken to prevent ecological destruction often choose to pursue covert active ecological resistance.

Unlike overt active ecological resistance, covert activity is not aimed at bearing witness, personal growth, or public education. Instead it is more concerned with the goal of immediately stopping, or at least hindering, activity harmful to the natural environment.[9] The roots of covert active ecological resistance reside in the anti-industrial sabotage of nineteenth century Europe.[10] The modern version of anti-industrial activity includes the spiking of trees (with metal or ceramic nails) in areas slated for logging, thus reducing the trees' value as timber and making the cutting of these trees difficult and dangerous. Survey stakes have been removed from wilderness areas, delaying or preventing the construction of roads and buildings. Bulldozers, road graters, timber machines, and other industrial equipment have been burned or sabotaged to slow and discourage the destruction of natural ecosystems.

That these actions are not the spontaneous activity of unthinking vandals is evidenced by the degree of planning that goes into them. The targets of covert ecological resisters are chosen carefully, with maximum damage or public reaction in mind. In the case of tree spiking, many of these actions are done years in advance of actual threat to the ecosystem. As a result, few covert active ecological resisters are ever successfully prosecuted. Dave Foreman (1991, 112-16) advocates that covert active ecological resistance consciously strike at the economic realm, where marginally profitable ventures can be hurt the most. This successful strategy has driven up costs, led to the abandonment of ongoing projects, and discouraged the undertaking of new projects. Timber sales in Washington, Oregon, Virginia, New Mexico, and Montana have been stopped due to the economic disadvantages of harvesting spiked trees (Foreman 1991, 133-34). An appraisal of covert active ecological resistance published in 1990 suggests that covert direct action aimed at ecologically destructive economic targets is taking its toll nationwide, with the annual cost of ecotage to industry and government estimated at $20-25 million in national forests alone (C.M. 1990).

One of the main advantages of covert active ecological resistance is that it often succeeds in ecosystem preservation after overt praxis strategies have stalled, thus buying time for further overt strategies to be implemented. In one spectacular operation by two members of the Sea Shepherd Conservation Society, Iceland's plans to resume whaling (despite an international ban) were delayed due to $2 million in sabotage to a major whale processing plant and the sinking of half of Iceland's whaling fleet. Due to negative publicity and the threat of international boycotts, Iceland subsequently abandoned its whaling plans (Manes 1990, chap. 6; Scarce 1990, chaps. 6 and 11).

As in the Icelandic case, covert active ecological resistance is usually found in conjunction with overt active ecological resistance. Many Neo-Primitivists have found that a combination of the two praxis strategies is often more successful at stopping wilderness destruction than one tactic by itself. A case involving the destruction of a Hawaiian rain forest is a classic example. A company grinding up rain forest ohia for power-plant fuel was greatly hindered when ecoteurs firebombed a $250,000 wood chipper. Court action brought by overt active ecological resisters later revealed that the company had no permit for its operations. The company subsequently went bankrupt and its ecologically disruptive operations ceased (Foreman 1991, 134).

PRAXIS AND MYSTICAL DEEP ECOLOGY

Worldview Creation as Praxis

Julia Scofield Russell's "Evolution of an Ecofeminist" (1990), identifies one of the two main praxis orientations within Mystical Deep Ecology: concentration upon individual consciousness change as the method of creating one's preferred future. Russell maintains that lasting societal transformation can only begin, and end, with personal transformation. The praxis strategy that Russell advocates to achieve this transformation is meditation.

Russell's emphasis on meditation as a praxis strategy for consciousness change is typical of the praxis perspective of the Mystical Deep Ecologist. Mystical Deep Ecology argues that the caring and nurturing values that they seek to promote exist in the intuitive realm but are slighted and suppressed by the dominant worldview's emphasis on rationality. Mystical Deep Ecology's

praxis strategies thus stress bringing intuitive reality to the forefront of individual consciousness through the suppression of logical reasoning.[11]

Janet Biehl (1991) identifies a problem for Mystical Deep Ecology at this
point. Biehl maintains that if one relies upon individualized intuitions as a basis for reality and "shuts off" one's attempts to critically analyze and communi-
cate rationally, the recognition of "correct" or objective reality is indistinguish-
able from subjective perceptions (and misperceptions) of reality.[12] Chris Jones
(1989) provides an answer to this critique in his dissertation "*Gaia Futures:
The Emerging Mythology and Politics of the Earth.*" Jones describes Gaia Political Consciousness as a spiritually experienced, ecological, and feminist perception of the world stressing attunement with wilderness, sacred regard for all
life, respect for diversity, and an awe for existence (Jones 1989, 278). Jones
would see Biehl's critique of subjective misperception as being balanced by this
"political consciousness."

Jones identifies the goal for Mystical Deep Ecologist praxis as the
"propelling" of "this new cosmic story" into the collective consciousness. With
this analysis, Jones has laid out the basis of the second praxis orientation we
will discuss in this chapter, the attempts of Mystical Deep Ecologists to create
and legitimate an alternative view of reality in order to guide the intuitions of
their followers in the proper direction.

The Suppression of Reason and Development of Intuition

The need for individual consciousness change posited by Mystical Deep
Ecology centers around its critique of modernity. Since the Mystical Ecofeminist subgroup of Mystical Deep Ecology has refined this critique, this subgroup
is indicative of general Mystical Deep Ecology thought. Mystical Ecofeminists
claim that the growth of instrumental-objective reasoning has created a cosmology of domination that has led to the exploitation of women and nature and
is rapidly leading to the total destruction of the earth's biosphere.[13] Mystical
Ecofeminism sees the solution to this destruction in the active recognition and
development of one's feelings of empathy and compassion, the desire to nurture, and the sense of interconnectedness.[14] Spretnak (1989, 127-128) posits
that by focusing upon these intuitive messages from nature within one's body
one can experience a worldview that leads to peace, abandonment of the concept of otherness, and an ethics of mutual respect where moral conduct can
follow from one's moral identity. The praxis strategies that Mystical
Ecofeminism advocates in order to receive these intuitive messages from nature
call for the negation of the critical aspect of thinking that has typified rationality since the Enlightenment.[15] Orenstein (1990) sees this negation as positive.
Orenstein calls for Mystical Ecofeminism to adopt a praxis of endarkenment,
which she describes as a "bonding with the Earth and the invisible that will
reestablish our sense of interconnectedness with all things, phenomenal and
spiritual, that make up the totality of life in our cosmos."[16]

Praxis strategies undertaken to achieve this endarkenment include meditation, chanting, singing, dancing, drumming, and ritualistic activity from a variety of traditions (Christ 1990, 66; Merchant 1990, 101). Paula Gunn Allen
(1990, 52-57) adopts methods from Native American tribes to encourage an
awareness of interconnection with other forms of being through what she calls
"thinking with one's heart." Allen advocates singing "Heya-hey" to "each
shrub and tree, to each flower and vine, to each pebble and stone" and so on
until one has sung to "all the beings gathered on all the planes (Allen 1990, 55-
56)."[17] Allen believes this singing will enable one to connect to the loving,
caring, and nurturing aspects of the personality that the dominant Western
worldview discourages.

Mystical Ecofeminist Mara Lynn Keller (1990, 48-51) advocates the suppression of modern rationality through the reintroduction of ancient Greek
rituals such as the Eleusinian mysteries. Keller maintains that the fasting,
praying, and purification involved in these rituals present a "deeper" view of
reality than modern rationality by inducing "a special seeing, an opening of the
eyes" and a sense of universal connection, love, and transcendence (Keller
1990, 50).

Mystical Ecofeminists are not content merely to resurrect old ways of sup-
pressing rationality but also seek to create new methods as well. Joanna Macy,
a leading Buddhist writer, and Pat Fleming promote a ritual called the Council
of All Beings. They contend the Council of All Beings deepens one's understanding of the Mystical Deep Ecology by strengthening one's courage and
commitment to heal the earth. Although drumming, meditation, and ritualistic
cleansings are incorporated into the Council of All Beings, the primary feature
of the ritual is the suppression of the personalized self and the adoption of an
ecological persona other than that of human being (Fleming and Macy 1990,
95-98). The goal of this ritual is the negation of self to the point where one
"becomes" one's adopted persona, be it animal, vegetable, or mineral.

While the above rituals concentrate upon triggering specific aspects of the
Mystical Ecofeminist worldview, Deena Metzger (1989, 121-25) has created a
series of four rituals that she uses as a holistic introduction to the Mystical
Ecofeminist worldview. The first is a ritualized meditation focused upon the
development of empathy, or what Metzger believes furthers "knowing with
certainty the existence of another being" (Metzger 1989, 124). Two people sit
facing one another without speaking, looking in each other's eyes, for a period
of 20 to 40 minutes. The meditators are instructed beforehand to confront and
dissolve any feelings of superiority, distinction, or separation. This meditation
is used to invoke an awareness of otherness and a feeling of mutual comrade-
ship with fellow human beings.

The second meditation invokes the human/nature connection that Mystical
Ecofeminism centers upon. The meditator is led through various stages of
meditation where human identity is gradually dissolved and replaced by imag-
ining oneself as a tree. This is a common meditation used by Mystical

Ecofeminists, as the tree is seen as a sacred symbol representing connectedness, nurturing power, spirituality, and balance. The same feelings of empathy and mutualism established between human beings in Metzger's first meditation are now transferred to the natural world of nonhuman being.

The third meditation described by Metzger involves the maintenance of personal strength in times of doubt. With eyes closed, the meditators are told to imagine the sun being covered with dark clouds, but to maintain their focus upon and always imagine the light behind the clouds shining through. In this way the initiate is encouraged always to hold onto his or her faith, no matter what "darkness" or doubt may come.

In the fourth meditation, Metzger encourages nurturance, connectedness, and empathy through the adoption of a mothering role stressing personal care of diverse forms of otherness. One is told to allow images of everything one loves to fill one's mind and imagine oneself cradling and protecting these things. The meditation concludes with the earth as the last image cradled and protected. With these four meditations, Metzger has distilled the Mystical Ecofeminist worldview into a set of rituals that Metzger sees as forming a base for of a new ecofeminist-based religion.

The Creation of Mythology and the Mystical Deep Ecologist Worldview

The intuitive understanding of "how the world really is" that Mystical Ecofeminist rituals and meditations invoke cannot be proven rationally but must be accepted on faith.[18] Janet Biehl (1991, 89-90) has described this as the delegation of reality to the private realm where it cannot be communicated to anyone who does not share the faith. This presents a problem for Mystical Ecofeminism. Intuitive wisdom that Mystical Ecofeminism might call pathological can be claimed to be as legitimate as the intuitive experiences that Mystical Ecofeminism values.[19] To counter this conflict of intuitions, Mystical Deep Ecologists seek to legitimize their worldview through praxis strategies involving the creation of supporting myths and alternative versions of history.[20]

The most common of the supporting myths told by Mystical Deep Ecologists are those of Gaia, the Mother Earth goddess, and the peaceful, ecologically benign, matrifocal societies that worshipped her. Riane Eisler's version of prehistory (1987, 1990) presents the story dominantly accepted by Mystical Ecofeminism. Eisler begins with the early Neolithic period in Europe, where she contends archaeological findings by Marjita Gimbutas, Nicolas Platon, and Merlin Stone provide evidence of a Mystical Ecofeminist golden age. Eisler states that the harmonious cultures that existed, living in mystical, ritualistic connection with all their surroundings, were destroyed by Indo-European invaders who worshipped a Sky God instead of an immanent earth goddess (Eisler 1990, 23-34). Although there is much evidence to refute Eisler's claims, she believes that a praxis strategy aimed at recreating the Mother Nature-worshipping society she has posited in prehistory will correct the problems she sees existing in modern society.[21]

Another interesting and important attempt at reality creation is Starhawk's (1987) reenvisioning of the origin of the universe in terms of a birthing process rather than a big bang. Brian Swimme, a teacher of cosmology and author of *The Universe Is a Green Dragon*, contends that Starhawk's reconception can free modern thinking from a violent way of thinking obsessed with weapons and explosions to one where children learn that all beings are their kin because of their common birth (Swimme 1990, 18-21).

The goal of these alternative histories and ways of viewing reality is the legitimation of the Mystical Ecofeminist worldview. To the Mystical Deep Ecologist, the ability of a story to support the kind of society Mystical Deep Ecology wishes to create is more important than historical accuracy or scientific observation. Devall and Sessions (1985, 151) confirm these observations with their statements that the most important aspect of the concept of Gaia as a living system is that the myth itself is comforting and involving, while the scientific facts concerning Gaia are limited, cold, and manipulative. Literature is treated by Mystical Deep Ecologists in a manner similar to their approach to science and history, with comforting revision taking precedence over predominantly accepted theories, interpretations, and texts. Spretnak, for example, has rewritten Greek mythology to make it more "prepatriarchic" by ignoring aspects such as abduction and rape.[22]

PRAXIS AND SOCIAL ECOLOGY

Social Ecology and the Transformation of Society

Using Isaak's (1987) analysis of political change strategies, one can identify two major praxis orientations within Social Ecology.[23] The first praxis orientation can be categorized as the radical approach since it calls for total systemic change. The radical approach primarily utilizes strategies typical of nonviolent oppositional politics. The second praxis orientation can be called the reformist approach. The reformist approach agrees that major changes in the system are needed but concentrates upon the gradual Greening of society through participation within the dominant systems of power.[24] The goal of both the reformist and the radical praxis approaches is the integration of nature and what Social Ecologists call "natural precepts" into the realm of human being.[25] Examples of these precepts include diversity, cooperation, and freedom. Social Ecologists posit that by utilizing these precepts of nature as a blueprint for human design, their visions of eutopia can be realized.

Social Ecology and Radical Political Transformation

The primary praxis strategy of Social Ecologists who adopt the radical approach is the creation of institutions and participation in activities outside of the dominant political system.[26] The theory behind this strategy is based upon the concept of dual revolutionary power, where counterinstitutions are organized to compete with and offer alternatives to official political institutions, economic systems, and cultural traditions. To accomplish this, Social Ecologist praxis stresses inclusiveness, communicative action, and structures with power residing at the lowest possible level.[27]

In the economic realm, Social Ecologist praxis strategies include attempts to break the stranglehold of corporations on small communities and their workers by establishing nonprofit community-managed and community-owned food and merchandise cooperatives. These are viewed as a transition stage leading to a total economy of workplace democracies owned and managed by workers.[28] Social Ecologists have attempted to reduce their dependence upon the federal monetary system by establishing barter networks called Local Exchange Trading Systems.[29] To reduce the power of those seeking only profit from small communities, some Social Ecologists have organized community land trusts where local people buy and then manage land and businesses for the good of the entire community (Rohter 1992, chap. 5). The eventual goal of these economic praxis strategies is not only freedom from the dominant economic system but the development of a consciousness of community citizenship and mutual obligation. This municipalization of the local economy is seen as a means to politicize the economic realm and dissolve it into the civic domain (Bookchin 1986b).

Radical Social Ecologist praxis in the political realm has the goal of citizen empowerment. It attempts to do away with professional politicians and to redemocratize government in the spirit of Athenian democracy and New England town hall meetings (Barber 1984; Bookchin 1985a). Radical Social Ecologist praxis strategies encourage the creation of neighborhood assemblies and alternative citizen legislatures to push agendas from the grassroots (Kassman 1989a; Rohter 1992, chaps. 8 and 11). Bookchin advocates that these alternative community-based institutions form confederations and begin to challenge the powers and functions of the present governmental system.[30] Ernest Callenbach (1989) has gone so far as to outline a general strategy for these small, politically empowered communities to use as a guide to disassociate from the United States.[31]

Active attempts by radical Social Ecologists to integrate the natural world into alternative communities include Bill Mollison's attempts at self-sufficient communities practicing "permanent agriculture" (Mollison 1988, 149-54). Mollison has designed eco-villages of 30 to 200 houses with the goal of being totally independent of outside support. Peter Berg and the Planet Drum Foundation (1989), John Todd and Nancy Todd of the New Alchemy Institute

(1984), and Ira Rohter of the University of Hawaii Department of Political Science (1992) have designed similar projects for the cities of San Francisco and New York and the state of Hawaii, respectively. These proposals include a breakdown of traditional city/nature barriers, with miles of fish-laden aqueducts and streams, sidewalk edible gardening, and the reintroduction of wild animals. While the most radical of their ideas have not been realized, these Green City programs have inspired numerous reformist changes and served to network important civic organizations around common goals.[32]

Cultural traditions are also actively challenged by radical Social Ecology. Within Social Ecologist organizations, dominantly accepted and semiaccepted cultural beliefs such as racism, ageism, patriarchy, and heterosexuality have been challenged by the formation of the Green Justice Caucus, the Youth Green Network, the Women's Leadership Network, and the Lesbian, Gay and Bisexual Caucus. These radical networks seek to break the hierarchical grip on power they see being held by old, wealthy, white men by ensuring that alternative voices (and votes) are heard on all deliberations. Other Green groups, such as the Hawaii Green Movement, have institutionalized gender-balanced leadership roles from their inception and actively seek out people of color in order to break the grip of traditionally dominant elites (Kassman 1986; Slaton 1992, 99-104).

Social Ecology and Social Reform

The second praxis orientation that Social Ecologists follow in their attempt to restructure society is reformist in that it advocates active participation in the dominant institutions of society in an attempt to subvert from within. The most obvious of these attempts is the formation of Green political parties organized to run candidates for political office.[33] A less obvious but more traditional method of electoral participation is for Greens to run as Green Democrats and Green Republicans.[34] Participating in public hearings, referendum drives, and lobbying are other ways reformist Greens work within the political system.[35]

Outside of the electoral arena, Green reformists operate in large governmental bureaucracies and educational institutions attempting to Green these institutions from the inside out.[36] In the economic realm, Green reformists have set up Green Investment Funds, Green Banks, and Green Credit Unions advocating socially responsible investing.[37] The advocacy of socially responsible investing is typified by Greens in Portland, Oregon, who have started a community investment fund to sponsor a mixed-income cohousing community and a transitional house for women recovering from drug and alcohol abuse. Reform-minded Greens have also set up businesses and manufacturing companies touting everything from mechanisms to improve automobile gas mileage to Green disposable diapers (Plant and Plant 1991, 414). Slickly printed corporate magazines appealing to Green readers have also proliferated: *Garbage, Buzzworm,* and *In Business, the Magazine for Green Entrepreneurs.* On the high-tech front, Green computer networks and bulletin boards are readily accessible, and a Green television network has begun organizing in Chicago.

On the cultural integration front, reformist Social Ecologists try to combine public awareness, community rebuilding, and personal empowerment in their attempts to combat racism, sexism, and hierarchy. Examples include local Green groups nationwide who helped to organize and participated in Detroit Summer, a project that brought together activists from across the nation with people from "the Hood" in order to help rehabilitate one of America's most devastated inner cities (The Detroit Summer Coalition 1992). Syracuse Greens undertook a similar project, linking inner-city solidarity with ecology to highlight the problem of violence against children. The Demmy Project, in Syracuse, now plants a tree every time a child is killed in the community ("Local Green Updates," Summer 1992).

Other attempts to make human space more ecological include solar-power education and composting demonstrations, inner-city and rooftop gardening projects, the transformation of parking lots into parks, and the implementation of recycling programs. John and Nancy Todd (1984) have designed solar-powered bioshelters that feature greenhouses and aquaculture and are designed to be as self-sufficient as possible in energy and food. With ecological designs like the Todds' bioshelters readily available, people can choose the option to join the dominant economic system or, to a large extent, "opt out." Murray Bookchin is also helping people choose a more reformist path to social change. Bookchin has created a master of arts degree in Social Ecology in affiliation with Goddard College. At his Institute for Social Ecology, students learn the design, construction, and maintenance of eco-technologies such as windmills and solar collectors. Over two thousand students have participated in seminars granting college credit at the Institute (Institute for Social Ecology 1987-1994).

SUMMARY

Each of the three subcultures of the American Green movement participates in traditional political change activities. Each subculture also concentrates on changing political and cultural action in its own unique way. These praxis orientations spring from the cosmological underpinnings explored in the last chapter. Neo-Primitivism emphasizes active ecological resistance—both overt and covert. Mystical Deep Ecology stresses the creation of new ways of thinking. Its praxis is oriented toward worldview creation and the development of ecological intuition. Social Ecology encourages methods often used by social change activists, from reformism to the building of alternative institutions countering and replacing the functions performed by present power holders.

NOTES

1. See Bettina Huber's "Images of the Future," in *The Procedures of Futures Research*, ed. Jib Fowles (Westport, CT: Greenwood Press, 1978), 187 and Jim Dator's "Decolonizing the Future," in *The Next 25 Years*, ed. Andrew Spekke (New York: World Future Society, 1975), 14 for further discussion of transition strategies and their importance to the field of future studies.

2. See Rik Scarce's *The Eco-warriors* (Chicago: The Noble Press, 1990), Chris Manes's *Green Rage* (Boston: Little, Brown, 1990), and David Foreman's *Confessions of an Eco-Warrior* (New York: Harmony Books, 1991).

3. By proactive I mean taking initiative and suggesting or seeking to impose change rather than merely reacting to change imposed by others. Examples include the Earth First! proposal to expand wilderness versus simple protest against the destruction of wilderness.

4. I use Andrew Dobson's distinction between ecologism and environmentalism, spelled out in Dobson, *Green Political Thought* (Boston: Unwin Hyman, 1990).

5. Chris Manes (1990a) describes the difference between overt versus covert active ecological resistance in terms of civil disobedience versus ecotage in *Green Rage*, chapters 9 and 10. David Foreman (1991) describes the differences between the two praxis orientations in *Confessions of an Eco-Warrior* (pp. 130-31 and 169-70).

6. Chris Manes (1990a, 169) cites the Peaceful Direct Action Code, which many overt active ecological resistance advocates affirm before their activities as evidence of the values cited in the main text. Five points are invoked in this pledge, including an attitude of openness, friendliness, and respect; restraint from violence; restraint from property damage; refusal to carry weapons; and the pledge not to run.

7. David Foreman (1991) tells the story of his encounters with the FBI (161-63) and cites incidents where ecological activists have been threatened, injured, and murdered (125-28). Chris Manes (1990a, 193-208) cites further examples of retaliation against ecological activists including, the incident where agents of the French government blew up the Greenpeace ship, Rainbow Warrior, and killed a Greenpeace photographer.

8. The newest tactic of those who seek to harass overt active ecological resisters is the Strategic Lawsuit Against Public Participation, or SLAPP suit. Professors Penelope Canan and George Pring believe their study of these suits, "Strategic Lawsuits Against Public Participation" (*Social Problems*, no. 35, December 1988), show that thousands of civil actions are brought against citizens each year to discourage public protest and punish those who have exercised their political rights.

9. The five goals of Earth First!, for example, have been stated as stopping wilderness destruction now, (re)establishing large wilderness areas, reversing the growth of human population, reducing consumption, and taking individual action (David Foreman, "Now's the Time," *Mother Jones*, April/May 1990, 41).

10. Many Earth First! members proudly call themselves neo-Luddites and express this heritage through anti-industrial activity. Dave Foreman (1991, 34) links the origins of the EF! tactic of monkeywrenching, or ecotage, to the inspiration of Dutch workers who threw their wooden shoes, called sabots, into the gears of early industrial machines, thus creating the term sabotage. See also Tokar (1987, 89).

11. Mystical Deep Ecologists argue that this suppression of the analytic mind allows "truer" perceptions of reality to appear.

12. For more information, see Janet Biehl's *Rethinking Ecofeminist Politics* (Boston: South End Press, 1991), 81-104.

13. Charlene Spretnak claims this cosmology of domination is due to instrumental-objective reasoning's partial, fragmented, and alienating view of reality in her book *The Spiritual Dimension of Green Politics* (Santa Fe, NM: Bear, 1986), 27-29. Brian Swimme, agreeing with Spretnak in his article "How to Heal a Lobotomy" (in Diamond and Orenstein 1990, 16), compares the standard scientific training typifying this world-view to a frontal lobotomy, where emotions are severed and only a sliver of the original mind is left operative. Susan Griffin maintains that the sliver of mind that is left in Swimme's analogy embodies the worst of human tendencies and is oriented toward controlling, distancing, calculating and dominating, which in turn lead to social exploitation and ecological destruction (Griffin 1990, 87-99).

14. For Charlene Spretnak, author of several Mystical Ecofeminist books and a founder of the American Green movement, intuitive recognition means understanding "the true nature of being" through accessing "the subtle, suprarational reaches of the mind" (Spretnak 1986, 41).

15. See Jurgen Habermas, *The Theory of Communicative Action* (Boston: Beacon Press, vol. 1, 1984, and vol. 2, 1987) for an in-depth discussion of Enlightenment rationality.

16. Gloria Feman Orenstein, "Artists as Healers," in Diamond and Orenstein (1990), 280-82. Orenstein sees "nonverbal communication with sacred sites in nature" as a primary method of achieving this endarkenment. I assume she means silent meditation when she uses the term nonverbal communication, although she also advocates nature sculpting.

17. Paula Gunn Allen offers further examples in her article "The Woman I Love Is a Planet, The Planet I Love Is a Tree," in Diamond and Orenstein (1990), 55-56.

18. According to the ecofeminist witch Starhawk, "The mysteries of the absolute can never be explained—only felt or intuited" (Starhawk, *The Spiral Dance* [San Francisco: Harper & Row, 1979], 25).

19. A good example of "right" versus "wrong" intuitions (in the ecofeminist view) is offered by Spretnak (1986, 51, note), who maintains that positive intuitions or "body parables" occur primarily in women. Spretnak maintains that the majority of men's experiencing of "body parables" is unpleasant, leaving men feeling vulnerable and fearful.

From personal experience as a man, I must doubt Spretnak's statements. The question then arises as to whose intuitions and perceptions are wrong, Spretnak's or mine? Spretnak skirts this issue by automatically assuming men's intuitions are negative.

20. Gloria Feman Orenstein (1990, 286) calls this literature "medicine stories," and claims they connect the Mystical Ecofeminist to power through their lessons of "healing."

21. Janet Biehl (1991, 29-39) disputes Eisler's archaeological interpretations and contention that nature goddess-worshipping societies were any less oppressive than present society. This is discussed further in chapter 5.

22. Charlene Spretnak's *Lost Goddesses of Early Greece* (Boston: Beacon, 1981), 103-10, concerns the retelling of the myth of Demeter and Persephone. By seeking to control the dominant interpretations of reality, Mystical Ecofeminists thus hope to control individual intuitions concerning reality.

23. Alan Isaak's *An Introduction to Politics* (Glenview, IL: Scott, Foresman, 1987, 287-91) discusses social change categories in detail. Also see Samuel Huntington's *Political Order in a Changing Society* (New Haven, CT: Yale University Press, 1968) for an overview of political and social change categorization.

24. Green radicals often disagree with Green reformism, accusing reformationists of co-optation and activity that soothes one's conscience more than it changes society. Green reformists respond that Green radicalism is unrealistic and unnescessarily adversarial. For active discussions of the advantages and disadvantages of Green radicalism versus reform, see John Resenbrink's *The Greens and the Politics of Transformation* (San Pedro, CA: R & E Miles, 1992); Jay Walljasper's "Can Green Politics Take Root in the US?" (*Utne Reader*, [September/October 1989]: 142-43); and various authors under the broad topic title, "shades of Green" (*Utne Reader*, [July/August 1990]: 50-63).

25. Social Ecology believes that the new sciences of evolutionary biology, quantum physics, and ecology offer a "more true" view of the world than traditional science because these new sciences tend to posit nature as a balanced system stressing interconnectedness, participation, and process. See Fritjov Capra, *The Turning Point* (New York: Bantam Books, 1982), 75-97; Nancy Todd and John Todd, *Bioshelters, Ocean Arks, City Farming* (San Francisco: Sierra Club Books, 1984), 9 and 14-18; and Chris Maser, *The Redesigned Forest* (San Pedro, CA: R & E Miles, 1988) for overviews. Social Ecologists translate the characteristics of the new sciences into ecological precepts, which they then use as guides for the political restructuring of modern society.

26. Existing institutions are viewed as unwilling and unable to institute the fundamental changes that radical Social Ecologists seek. See Youth Green Caucus, *May 1989 Gathering Summary* (pages 7-9), for the rationale behind this view.

27. See Biehl (1991, 150-157) for one Social Ecologists view of an ideal structure for what she calls "a new political realm."

28. See Ira Rohter, *A Green Hawai'i*, (Honolulu: Na Kane O Ka Malo Press, 1992), 107-21, for an in-depth discussion of Green co-ops and workplace democracies. Tokar's *The Green Alternative* (San Pedro, CA: R and E Miles, 1987), 108-12, offers good historical background and additional contemporary case studies.

29. See Michael Linton and Thomas Greco, "LETS: The Local Exchange Trading System," in Van Andruss, Christopher Plant, Judith Plant and Eleanor Wright (1990), 155-58 for an overview of how these systems work. In the Berkshire Mountains of western Massachusetts, people affiliated with the E.F. Schumacher Society have gone so far as to establish a local currency based upon the value of a cord of firewood in order to remove themselves from the federal economic system and promote community. See Tokar (1987, 110).

30. Murray Bookchin, "Municipal Libertarianism," in Van Andruss, Christopher Plant, Judith Plant, and Eleanor Wright (1990), 145-46. For a critique of this proposal, see Mike Muench, "Some Politics for a Green Party," *Green Synthesis*, no. 36 (August 1992), 9-11.

31. Ernest Callenbach's *Ecotopia Emerging* (1989) begins with small communities issuing declarations of independence, citing local authority and laws as having legal force above federal and state laws. The county of Hawaii tried a version of this, through a citizen-sponsored official initiative, declaring itself a nuclear-free zone. The United States government promptly sent a warship suspected of carrying nuclear weapons into Hilo Harbor to show the locals who's boss. The leading advocate of the nuclear-free initiative, Jim Albertini, jumped into the harbor to protest the ship's arrival. He spent

three minutes swimming in the harbor, was arrested, and was sentenced to three years in a federal prison 1,500 miles from his home. This example illustrates the difficulties local activists will face in actualizing Callenbach's scenario.

32. One hundred and thirty-five citizen groups have endorsed the New York Green City Program (Andruss et al. 1990, 105). One hundred and fifty groups in San Francisco participated in the creation of a Green city program for San Francisco Bay area cities and towns (Peter Berg, Beth Magilavy and Seth Zuckerman, *A Green City Program for San Francisco Bay Area Cities and Towns* [San Francisco: Planet Books, 1989]).

33. Eighty-five Green candidates from thirteen states ran in the November 1992 elections; 13 of them won, making a total of 58 elected Greens in local and county positions throughout the United States (Chris Seymour, "Third Party Organizing," *Z Magazine* [November 1992]: 51; and Jodean Marks, "Proposal for a Green Electoral Politics Conference," *The Greens Bulletin* [December 1992]: 57).

34. In a survey of Green-oriented legislation introduced into the U.S. Congress, Carol Grunewald Rifkin came to the conclusion that 10 U.S. Senators and 39 Representatives could be considered "unofficial or proto-Greens." Leading the list was the vice-president, Al Gore. Of these 49 legislators, only 2 Republicans made the list. See Rifkin's "The Greening of Capital Hill" (*Utne Reader* no. 53 [September/October 1992]: 99).

35. See "Local Green Updates," *Green Politics* 2, no. 2 (Summer 1992): 3-4), for current examples by local Green groups. Also see Seth Zuckerman, "A Grassroots Rebellion Revamps Environmentalism" (*Utne Reader* no. 21 [May/June 1987]: 76-79), for a good discussion of the pitfalls and successes of these approaches.

36. One of the best examples of ecological reformists working inside a government organization is the dissident Forest Service employees who publish *Inner Voice*. These employees call themselves The Association of Forest Service Employees for Environmental Ethics and demand radical change in Forest Service policies and procedures. At the University of Hawai'i there were more than one dozen Green activists teaching at the major campuses and community colleges when I taught there in the late eighties and early nineties.

37. See Susan Meeker-Lowry, "Breaking Free: Building Bioregional Economies," in *Turtle Talk,* ed. Plant and Plant (Philadelphia: New Society, 1990), 114-123. Rohter (1992, 414, n. 53) maintains that socially responsible investing reached $625 billion in 1990.

Green Visions of Eutopia   *4*

This chapter explores eutopianism within the preferred futures of the three cosmological subcultures of the American Green movement. Neo-Primitivism, Mystical Deep Ecology, and Social Ecology all put forth visionary images of radical transformation leading to what they consider to be ideal future societies. Some observers term these visions utopian: defining any Green preferred future as "a visionary, impractical scheme for social improvement" or "the depiction of some nonexistent society representing ideal perfection."[1] Others, such as Brian Tokar (1987, 55-56), maintain that Green visions are not impractical dreams but comprehensive critiques of the present that inspire the creation of new political and social forms. The transformational images of the future envisioned by the three subcultures of the American Green movement can thus be viewed two ways: (1) as the impractical "no places" of utopian literature, or (2) as models for reachable and preferable future societies.

Perhaps both of these categories are incomplete. It is unlikely that any of the Green utopias outlined below will come into existence as envisioned by their proponents. Yet the future visions of the various subcultures of the Green movement have sparked movements for major political and social change in countries around the world.[2] As guiding images of the future used to orient action toward a set of long-range goals, Green visions should not be called utopias but are better classified as eutopias: feasible and desirable futures that people can and do strive to create.[3] Eutopian images are important because they actively encourage and motivate political and social change activity. Jim Dator (1974a), Pierre Bertaux (1968), and Eleonora Masini (1982) have all made the point that it is through images of desirable futures that the direction of the present is determined. Burt Nanus (1990) takes an even stronger position by positing such images as the basis of leadership.

The preferable "good societies" posited by Neo-Primitivists, Mystical Deep Ecologists, and Social Ecologists have the potential to create great changes in American (and world) politics. These Green eutopias deserve examination to determine what life might actually be like in these possible futures. This chapter approaches the analysis of Green eutopias (as compiled from the composite writings of major subculture theorists) from two methodological positions. First, a scenario illustrating several hours in the life of a typical member of the future society is presented.[4] The point of the scenario is to offer a montage of the subculture's future values, customs, environmental relationships, and social structures in mutual interaction. The form of the scenario presentation is intended to allow the reader to "get inside the heads" of subculture advocates and present as realistically as possible what the people in these preferred future societies might think, feel, and value.

The second approach used in this chapter concentrates upon "incasting," or deductive forecasting, a methodological tool developed by Jim Dator, the Institute for Alternative Futures, and the Alternative Futures Option of the Department of Political Science, University of Hawaii (Jones 1989, 261; Schultz 1991, 202). Incasting is used to expand upon the scenarios by penetrating more deeply into the philosophical, cultural, and structural differences existing between the three Green subcultures. Incasting accomplishes this by projecting specific aspects of reality, such as the need for government, into a matrix of Green values. Each element cast into the matrix will take form in accordance with each subculture's worldview. The differences among the subculture future eutopias are presented below. Categories relating to the four major values of the international Green movement (ecological harmony, social justice, democratic participation, and nonviolence) are used to group the results. Table 6 in appendix A offers an overview of the incasting matrix and its results.

THE NEO-PRIMITIVIST FUTURE VISION

Introduction

The Neo-Primitivist eutopia emphasizes the rejection of technology and the return to a simpler, less civilized time and way of being.[5] There are no cars, no compact disk players, no video games, no blow-dryers, no MTV. In fact, there is no electricity in the Neo-Primitivist future. There are a few areas of permanent habitation, but no cities. Technology is rudimentary and tools are handmade. Food is primarily hunted and gathered. Agriculture is looked upon as the unnatural manipulation of nature. It is unlikely that one would find many domesticated animals in this future, given its emphasis on the free and the wild.

This eutopia is so unlike any continuation of the present that the most probable way such a future could occur is by a collapse of the present civilizational system similar to the collapse that left the Mayan civilization in shambles.[6] It is an essential element of Neo-Primitivist ideology that such systemic collapse is ultimately probable and should be encouraged at every opportunity.[7]

Models for the Neo-Primitivist future focus upon the long precivilizational and preagricultural period of human society. Most Neo-Primitivists accept William Glasser's arguments that the 500,000 years preceding the invention of agriculture were relatively peaceful and abundant: a time where focus on individual identity triumphed over material concerns.[8]

The Neo-Primitivist Eutopian Scenario

Donna Falcon Free, "Falc" to her friends, Falcon to the elders, bolted upright from her bed of cedar boughs. Adrenaline pumped through her veins, and her heart was beating wildly. Falcon's head glanced swiftly back and forth, scanning the animal hide shelter that protected her family from the elements.

"The Dream," she thought "I've had the Dream again. Surely, the hunting party will take me with them now."

Falcon knew the Dream well, or should one call it the Vision? Whatever term one used, Falcon knew the significance and truth contained within the shifting spectral images that had now visited her three nights in a row. The dream started ordinarily enough. Falcon found herself wandering through the grassy plain lands to the northeast of her tribe's encampment. Over her shoulder Falcon carried her spear nonchalantly, felt the slight wind on her cheek, and studied the dark blue sky over the rolling hill ahead. As Falcon neared the crest of the hill, she became wary, feeling the presence of the many beings beyond. Crouching, the spear now steady in her hands, Falcon smelled the wind and knew what she had no need to see. Buffalo. It must be one of the smaller herds that now roamed the Northwest. Only twenty to thirty animals per grouping, these herds were no equal to the herds containing hundreds of buffalo that Falcon had been told now grazed the grasslands of the Midwest. Still, a Northwest herd contained enough meat to last her tribe a winter, enough hide to keep one warm and protected when need be, and enough bone and horn to make many fine ornaments and tools.

"Today, I have proved my worth to the village," thought Falcon as she descended the crest on her way back home.

Falcon was halfway down the small bluff when suddenly, from behind her back, she heard the most terrifying sound she had ever heard. It was high-pitched, almost like the whine of a rabbit caught in the jaws of a coyote. The scream was followed by a low rumble, not unlike the clearing of phlegm from a great, deep throat. Falcon knew these sounds were meant as a challenge. She turned quickly.

"So you, little one, would kill my people?" bellowed the biggest bull buffalo Falcon had ever seen. "Then, in self-protection, I must kill you." The buffalo snorted, lowered his mighty head, pawed the ground once, and then charged.

Falcon lifted the spear she had made with her own hands. The spear felt good and right. Falcon knew it flew true; she had thrown it a thousand times before. In practice. At pine cones, at squirrels and rabbits, at fish and at snakes. And now Falcon drew her shaking arm back to her shoulder and stared at the thundering face of death itself.

"Release, release!" screamed Falcon's mind as the horror grew nearer.

Falcon's arm steadied and swiftly moved forward. The spear flew, piercing the large bull's right eye and sinking deep into his brain. Tortured anguish ripped through the chief of the buffalo tribe, but only for a second. He fell without taking a further breath. The body of the mighty giant rolled with the force of momentum and stopped centimeters from Falcon's feet. Falcon let out a victory cry that echoed over the plain, sank to her knees, and asked forgiveness of the old buffalo. She then rose, cut the steaming liver from his hot body, and took a bloody bite.

"Now I am you, and you are me," said Falcon to the old bull. "We will both live on together."

"Greetings," said Falcon's father as he opened the flap of the teepee-like shelter.

"Dad, I had the Dream again," said Falcon.

"I know," replied her father, "And I have just come from the elders. The purification rituals are ready and we await your presence in the sweat lodge. Today you join the hunt. Today you become one of the few, those called to the role of the warrior."

Falcon knew the honor of what was to come. The warriors in her tribe did more than protect the people from their enemies when the occasional skirmishes that marked the area's primitive form of warfare broke out. Warriors were also mediators. They were the people's protection from internal domination as well as external. In Falcon's tribe individual freedom was of ultimate importance and the warriors made sure that the loose form of government accepted by the tribe stayed as limited as possible.

Falcon rose and followed her father past the tipilike tents which encircled the tribal commons. Tools lay here and there upon the ground, used by whoever needed them at the time and then left for others to use. Falcon and her Father walked past the cooking fires, past the blanket weavers and past the elder craftmakers. Falcon smiled at her friends, neighbors, and relatives as she walked.

"Everybody has a place and a duty," she thought.

Her own duties were very important, especially that of food gatherer, since the tribe eschewed agriculture (Falcon's tribe even refused to domesticate animals). Falcon soon arrived at the large circle of flame at the north end of the village encampment. Surrounding the flame were two dozen men and women, ages 16 to 45. Their faces and bodies seemed to be the living renditions of the Spirits of the Hunt, painted with the natural hues of charcoal, ocher, fungus, berries and blood. Behind the circle and directly to the north, with the tiny door facing directly to the south was the sweat lodge. A small river, fed by a towering glacier over one hundred miles to the northeast, ran behind the tiny circular hut. The sweat lodge was made of mud and branches and covered with woven mats. The tribal Great Hunters, two men and one woman who had recently rotated into the honorary positions, were dressed in the skins of departed animals. The skins were considered totems passed down from the Great Hunt of tribal legend, the most successful hunt in the tribe's history.

The Great Hunters invited Falcon into the circle and began to chant, smudging her with sage and asking the Spirits of the Hunt to accept Falcon as their newest warrior. In the distance Falcon heard the hiss of steam as the cooking fires were extinguished. There would be no fire in the encampment except for the ceremonial fire this night. No cooking was allowed, no craftwork, repairs or heavy labor was to be undertaken until the ceremony was completed. Falcon looked into the fire. She thanked the Stone People who had agreed to participate in her ritual. Without the stones, there would be no steam, and without the steam, no purification. Without purification there would be no atonement with the animals of the hunt. Bad luck would follow the entire village as the dishonored spirits sought to regain their self-respect. The Stone People were important participants in this ritual, as were the Fire, Water, Plant, and Tree people. By agreeing to participate, these peoples showed Falcon their blessing and their acceptance of her as warrior-to-be. Falcon thanked them all sincerely.

When the chanting was over, Falcon followed the Greatest of the Great Hunters into the sweat lodge. The entrance was low, so she crawled on her knees onto the cedar strewn floor of the sweat lodge and into the darkness, as did the Great Hunter before her and the Great Hunter after her. The flap to the sweat lodge was closed. Inside, the sweat lodge was black, blacker than she had ever seen (at least in her conscious memory). The Great Hunters asked Falcon to retell her Dream. While Falcon did, the Great Hunters listened respectfully and then began to chant. The flap of the sweat lodge opened and the rest of the tribal warriors entered. On their knees. One to the right of Falcon, one to the left, until the entire tent was so full it seemed no more would fit. Still, somehow more did.

The chanting by the Great Hunters continued. When the final warrior had entered the tent, eight large Stone People were passed in. They glowed red hot in the darkness and spit sparks as they were gently placed in the small depression in the center of the lodge. Heat immediately filled the tiny space already crammed full of sweaty bodies. The rocks in the center of the room pulsated with life. The Great Huntswoman thanked the Stone People, the Spirits of the Water and the Fire and the Cedar Spirits for their participation and cooperation. She began chanting and sprinkled a mixture of water and herbal medicine onto the rocks. Steam flew everywhere as scalding hot moisture suddenly filled the sweat lodge. One by one the other hunters began to sing their individual chants as the Great Huntswoman repeated her ritual blessing of the rocks. After what seemed like hours of praying, chanting, sweating, and almost blacking out in the unbearable heat and steam, the Great Huntswoman stopped. She motioned the door open, and a blast of cool air hit Falcon like a hammer.

The hunters filed out of the sweat lodge, on their knees, one by one, blinded by sudden sunlight. When Falcon emerged, the warriors gave a cheer, ran to the ice cold river, and jumped in. Falcon followed, feeling more dead, then more alive, than she had ever felt before. After the brief swim, the hunters gathered around the fire, gave thanks to the Four Directions, to the Gods of the Hunt, to the Chiefs of the Animal Tribes, to the Plant, Stone, Fire, and Water Peoples. The warriors then drank the ceremonial tea, offered to them by the Great Hunters and reentered the sweat lodge. This entire process of ritualization was repeated four more times, until it was late at night and the sunlight no longer stung the warriors' eyes when they emerged from their fiery burrow of purification.

Inside the sweat lodge, different chants, prayers, atonements, and revelations came by the hour. Before leaving the sweat lodge for the last time, all had become purified. All ears had heard Falcon's Dream. All souls listened to her prayer for forgiveness. All hearts searched and sang as Falcon found her own unique song. The hunters agreed by consensus that Falcon would lead the hunting party to the place in her dream at the first light of morning. Falcon emerged from the sweat lodge for the last time that night. She walked silently to the river, dove in, and emerged. She felt purified and reborn. Falcon had no fear of the morning to come, for she knew that her Vision was true. Falcon was meant to be and always would be a warrior.

Analysis of the Neo-Primitivist Eutopia

Ecological harmony in the Neo-Primitivist eutopia. The Neo-Primitivist future has the potential to be the most ecological of the futures posited by the three American Green subcultures. The emphasis in this future is upon keeping wilderness wild. Any attempt to domesticate natural wildness is discouraged. The focus on gathering food rather than farming illustrates the extent to which Neo-Primitivism is willing to go to limit the manipulation of nature.

Although hunting is allowed, which may seem problematic to Green animal rights activists, this expression of ecological interaction is highly limited through ritualization. Neo-Primitivists are careful to keep hunting within the limits of bioregional tolerances. As is the case today in cases of animal overpopulation, hunting in the Neo-Primitivist future is often seen as more ecologically benign than not hunting. Given the attunement to natural limits that many primal peoples have shown (such as establishing taboos on certain species during breeding times and periods when animals seem scarce), hunting could be viewed as violating the Green value of nonviolence more than the value of ecological harmony.[9]

In this scenario, the extent of negative ecological impact on any one place is limited because the Neo-Primitivist eutopian community is largely Paleolithic and nomadic. The anticapitalist, nonmaterialist, and extremely low-technology stance of the Neo-Primitivist further limits human impact on the ecosystem. In this future, people have effectively become part of the natural region they find themselves in. Ecological knowledge is valued above all other knowledge. While nature is not worshipped as a god or goddess, wilderness is seen as the site of spirituality, and thus it is sacred and worthy of respect. Like the other animals and plants of their bioregion, humans in the Neo-Primitivist future eutopia have adapted their lifestyle to fit their surroundings (Foreman 1991, 74; Sale 1985).

Social justice in the Neo-Primitivist eutopia. Community organization, personal identity and security in the Neo-Primitivist future is oriented around the tribe and the clan (Booth 1990, 73-74; Foreman 1990, 65). The tribe and clan take care of their own, providing help and support to one another in meeting basic needs. All share equally in the good times and all suffer equally in the bad. All resources and material items are shared communally, utilizing the concept of usufruct, where one takes or is naturally granted what one needs and the concept of private ownership is virtually nonexistent. What is important to this future society is not material wealth but personal dignity and worth to the community as a whole. Not only is the amassing of wealth frowned upon for being unecological and uncommunal, it is impractical in a nomadic society. Status is measured more by what one gives away than by what one possesses. Potlatches are yearly occurrences to redistribute wealth, gain status, and cement bonds.

Freedom (meaning the ability to be oneself, and relaxation of norms stressing social conformity) is cherished and encouraged in the Neo-Primitivist future eutopia. A combination of warrior and hunter is the role most honored, due to the required skills, social protection, and mythological history (relating the rise of the very first eco-warriors to the downfall of industrial civilization); however, all social positions are honored. It is recognized that every person is a positive contributor to society, including the insane. There is little gender stereotyping, and all social roles are open to all people.

Democratic participation in the Neo-Primitivist eutopia. Given the Neo-Primitivist emphasis on freedom and individual responsibility, government has an extremely limited role in this future eutopia.[10] The saying "No person can tell another what to do" is the basic law. The most common form of government is the consensual tribal meeting, where all who are affected by the outcome of a decision have a say in that decision. In all tribal decisions, individual compliance is strictly voluntary. This self-regulation includes participation in tribal sanctions. Compliance with communal decisions is given because one believes the decision is right or that general compliance is needed for the good of the group as a whole. Since tribal members are very interdependent and close-knit, it is rare that governmental decisions are out of synchronization with the will of the vast majority of the tribe.[11]

In large tribes, more than a few dozen people, the tribal council form of government is used. Tribal councils include representatives of recognized interest groups and familial clans of the tribe. When needed, the tribal council chooses a speaker to represent it in specific intertribal dealings. All leadership positions are task specific and limited as to scope and function. Tribal members value diversity and self-determination and as a result have many leaders. Although the best fisherman is usually the leader of the fishing parties, the best forager or cook is the leader of the gathering, and so on, these positions are often rotated to encourage learning (and develop empathy) among tribal members (Paige 1977, 1983).

Tribal disputes are decided by the tribe as a whole or by the persons most interested in the outcome. Emphasis is on individual freedom as well as tribal harmony. When individual self-control is broken, it is viewed as an individual or familial problem unless an act offends the tribe as a whole. Since the tribe is the basis of identity as well as life, expulsion from a tribe is the ultimate punishment.

Nonviolence in the Neo-Primitivist eutopia. Violence is recognized as an inherent part of nature and an inevitable part of humanity in the Neo-Primitivist future (Foreman 1990, 63). This violence seldom includes violence toward other human beings, but is more survival oriented and directed at animals. Acts such as the eating of a raw but still hot and steaming liver from an animal one has just killed may seem savage to modern perceptions, but such acts are very different from striking out of wanton or planned aggression, a behavior one associates with modern violence.

Structural violence is virtually unknown in the Neo-Primitivist future eutopia. Since self-control is a valued norm in these anarchistic societies, when violence toward other humans does occur, it is immediate, in the heat of passion, and quickly over. Although skirmishes or "wars" between tribes occur, they are of limited scope and duration and highly ritualized. The violence of these conflicts takes place away from tribal encampments and involves only trained warriors. Viewed in the context of modern conflict, social life in the Neo-Primitivist future eutopia could be considered much more secure and less violent than life in most large American cities today.

The killing of animals constitutes the primary violence in the Neo-Primitivist eutopia. Hunting is viewed as a necessary and important part of tribal culture. Elaborate rituals have been developed, however, to control the violence inherent in hunting.[12] As in the scenario above, fasting, dancing, chanting, and praying to the many spirits that are believed to inhabit the world are used before violence is undertaken. These rituals are not to ensure a successful hunt but rather are an atonement to the individual animals which must be killed. Similar rituals are enacted after the violence has occurred to make right that which the hunt has unbalanced. The belief that spirits reside in all being and that these spirits can affect oneself limits the exploitation of animals, plants and inanimate nature.

THE MYSTICAL DEEP ECOLOGY FUTURE VISION

Introduction

The eutopia presented in this section focuses upon the ecofeminist aspects of Mystical Deep Ecology. The ecofeminist scenario is more descriptive of the Gaia-centered cosmological orientations of the subculture than scenarios taking a noncritical approach toward gender.[13] Taken to its logical conclusions, it is the Mystical Ecofeminist interpretation of Gaia from which the three prime foci of the Mystical Deep Ecology future culture emerge: (1) a matriarchal orientation toward social structure, (2) a religious-metaphysical orientation toward ontology and epistemology, and (3) an ecological eutopian (ecotopic) reverence toward the natural world.[14]

The comforting image of a divinely immanent Earth Mother has become the center of Mystical Deep Ecology's cosmology.[15] The preferred future that Mystical Deep Ecology looks to is based upon models of a mystical, matrifocal, peaceful, and agrarian past, "a time when the wisdom of the mother was honored above all" (Eisler 1990, 27).

The Mystical Deep Ecology Eutopian Scenario

Jeff loved life in Fir City. While not a real city, at least not like the cities the elders spoke of in their mythological stories, Fir City was the biggest settlement in the bioregion of Cascadia. With over 3,000 people in his hometown, Jeff imagined it must be one of the largest cities in the world. At least in the known world. Trips to the world outside the bioregion were pretty well limited to the immediate surrounding bioregions of Ish and Sage. Communication was equally limited. After all, why bother with outsiders? Cascadia was self-sufficient. It produced enough to meet what little material needs its people required—and was proud of it. The fertile soil and temperate climate surrounding Fir City made it rich in foodstuffs and the natural materials needed for the clothing, housing, and light manufacturing done in Cascadia. The area was rich in beauty as well. The intensive penetrations of the ecosystem (mining, oil drilling, clear-cut forestry, highways, and large cement buildings, for example) tolerated by previous ages were not outlawed. Nature was watched closely for signs that Gaia approved of the way human beings treated her many component parts. Wildlife was abundant due to the religious prohibitions against killing any form of life. Cascadia even had enough villages so Cascadians could intermarry without fear of limiting the gene pool, so why leave one's family and homeland for any reason?

Jeff lived in the house where his mother had been raised. And her mother before her. In fact, all three generations still lived together in the large wooden house nestled between Fir Forest and Trout Lake. Jeff was sad to think that some day he would have to leave the home of his ancestors, but that was the way it was. Men who married were required to move in with the wife's family in this matrilineal society. Jeff envied his sister, who would inherit the house and use of the surrounding land, but when he thought about his sweetheart, Birgit his envy was replaced by a stronger emotion, love. Although he was only 14, he had known Birgit all his life. At first, she was just the older girl across the lake, who would take him on walks and teach him the things about life he needed to know. Since Birgit was now 18, the time was fast approaching when Jeff and she would wed, as their mothers had decided more than 10 years before.

The age difference between the two youths was usual in Cascadia. Males needed an older and wiser women to teach them the proper ways of life, and it was common for boys to have such a mentor before they became toddlers. When both children became older, the roles would continue as they became marriage partners. The role of the young female mentors was not an easy one. Boys had to be taught to control their aggression, their loudness and craziness. They had to be shown how to listen to the voice of the Earth, the Mother Goddess, and obey her wisdom. Most of all, they had to be taught how to love, cherish, and nurture. It was often tough work, but most mentors loved their duty and most of the young boys worshipped their mentors.

Jeff was still thinking about his love for Birgit and all she had taught him when he saw his friend Sasha paddling his small canoe toward the backyard.

"Ready to do some weaving?" shouted Sasha.

"Got the looms all set up," answered Jeff. "Were you able to get the goldenrod dye?"

"Yup, my father had some left over from the Equinox, but we have to replace it by New Moon. He wants to make a special umbrella for mom before the rains start," said Sasha.

Jeff helped Sasha tie up the canoe at the little dock behind the house. "I've got the design for Birgit's blanket all scoped out," he said to Sasha. "Come on, check this out."

The boys ran up to the house, where the looms were set on the large deck facing the lake. "Wow," said Sasha, looking at the multicolored design on the piece of paper Jeff eagerly showed him, "Wish I could imagine stuff like that."

"Ah, with someone like Birgit to inspire me, it was easy," said Jeff modestly. "Actually," he continued, "this is the story of our first real sexual encounter."

Sasha nodded solemnly. He had expected as much.

"The dark blue in the blanket here represents the lake, over by Porcupine Peak."

"I knew it," interrupted Sasha. "And the green running past is Seven Deer Meadow."

Jeff laughed. "Ya, guess I'm not the first one to partake of the sacrament there. It really is such a holy spot. I was one with the grass, and the soil, and the trees. The trees were so magnificent. The sky was diamonds, Sasha, diamonds. And the dandelions. Sasha, that was why I wanted the goldenrod so badly. I swear the dandelions reached right into my soul and grabbed it! There I was, flat on my back, feeling that delicious warmth the summer soil gives you from below and that the hot July sun gives us from above. I rolled over and looked at Birgit's mane of yellow hair and then into those golden eyes, and they transmuted. Just like in the holy texts. Those glorious eyes turned right into dandelions, Sasha. I thought it was a reflection from the meadow at first, but then those dandelion eyes sucked me in, and I knew it was all true. Gaia lives in each one of us, Sasha. Birgit was a dandelion. I became the dandelion in her eyes. There were a million shining brother and sister dandelions dancing all around us singing praises to Gaia. You were there, Sasha. And so was Mom and Dad and Sis and Grandma and everyone. And that is what I need the goldenrod dye for. In every speck of the blue and the green and the brown and the gray of our wedding blanket there will be a little goldenrod. And the two brightest spots of all will be smack in the center of the blanket, to represent the day that the center spoke to me. Mother Gaia through Birgit's eyes. The day of my enlightenment."

Analysis of the Eutopian Potential of Mystical Deep Ecology

Ecological harmony in the Mystical Deep Ecology eutopia. The Green criterion of ecological harmony and the philosophical stance of nonviolence toward nature are the most highly emphasized values within the Mystical Deep Ecology eutopia. The Mystical Deep Ecologist future culture worships the earth as its mother and the life upon it as its sacred kin. This religious-metaphysical perspective is coupled with the concept of biocentric egalitarianism to produce the cosmological foundation for the argument that instrumental use of the earth and the creatures upon it be highly restricted. The religious-metaphysical worship of earth as mother further promotes a detailed attention to one's environmental surroundings. Since Gaia is immanent in all, one does not want to offend the Goddess through exploitative or disrespectful action toward one of her many manifestations.

The Mystical Deep Ecology eutopia thus stresses a highly aware, low-impact, environmentally benign lifestyle. The high level of environmental awareness is evident, as nature is constantly watched for signs or messages from Gaia (Kassman 1989c, 1990b). The low-impact consciousness translates into a low-technology, "conserver" society (Dator 1979; Jones 1989; Valaskakis

1979). To stress the benign nature of this society, ecologically unavoidable manipulations of the earth are geared to "put more back than one takes" (Jones 1989, 239). Agriculture thus replenishes rather than depletes the soil (Rohter 1992, Chaps. 4, 5, and 9).

Mystical Deep Ecologists argue that it is the compassion they show for the earth and its creatures that puts Mystical Deep Ecology a step ahead of the ecological philosophy of noninterference posited by the Neo-Primitivists (Starhawk 1989). Hospitable environmental wilderness areas have been established for the flourishing of flora and fauna. Hunting and raising animals for food is forbidden, for it is seen in the same light as war and human cannibalism are seen today. Some limited free-ranging domestication of cattle and poultry is allowed for milk and eggs, but the entire society is primarily vegetarian. Clothing and other items made from animals, including fur and leather, are prohibited, but limited wool production is tolerated. Zoos are outlawed, being viewed as animal slavery, although personal "companion animals" are permitted. Companion animals are not thought of as being owned by a person as property but are seen as individuals who have freely chosen to live with humans and who may freely choose to leave.[16] Mystical Deep Ecologists see themselves as stewards, protectors, and enhancers of Gaia's gift of life.

Social justice in the Mystical Deep Ecology eutopia. Ethnographic studies suggest that the early Neolithic horticultural societies that Mystical Deep Ecologists posit as models for their preferred futures were basically gender egalitarian, with the status of women much higher than in later civilized societies (Biehl 1991, 31). More recent models discussed by Mystical Deep Ecologists, such as the matrilineal Iroquois of North America, depict a society where women controlled the distribution of food and wealth, nominated and could depose tribal chiefs, and had a voice in all questions brought before the tribe (Leacock 1987, 28). Goods in graves of matrifocal societies were found to be very limited and of equal quality and quantity, thus suggesting a nonmaterialist and egalitarian culture (Ehrenberg 1989, 95-99). Utilizing ethnographic research, historical anthropology, the theories of twentieth-century mystical ecofeminists, and the feminist utopian novels of the nineteenth-century, the Mystical Deep Ecologists in Cascadia adopted a matrifocal partnership model for their society.[17]

The official religion of Cascadia is the worship of Gaia as the Mother Goddess. As religion permeates every aspect of life in this eutopia, a matrifocal society is seen as a natural step in the evolution of society for the Cascadians.[18] Men and women share societal tasks fairly equally in this future, although jobs requiring nurturing and connection to the earth are primarily reserved for men, with women as guides or overseers. Both genders know that men need extra practice in these areas due to their innate biological weakness of being born male.[19] Since the nonmaterialistic motto of "live lightly upon the Earth" is supreme, there really is not much work to be done. Most of the daily chores consist of tending the small fields and gathering places, taking care of the house and surroundings, and cooking the meals. Institutions such as usury, money lending, and the wage slavery associated with capitalism are outlawed. The means of production are communally owned, and usufruct is the rule. If one participates in a project, then one shares the results according to one's needs. Each household is basically self-sufficient, although strong kinship ties make communalist cooperation and sharing commonplace. Some light crafts exist, such as glassmaking, but the practitioners are actually teachers, helping others to make their own products. In times of accident or disaster, each household is linked into two larger communities. The first is kinship oriented, following lineage on the mother's side. The second is religious, similar to the parish or ward, where all members serve one another as needed.

Democratic participation in the Mystical Deep Ecology eutopia. The partnership society of the Mystical Deep Ecologist future allows democratic participation by both genders; however, the ontological connection of the female to Gaia gives women some very special political responsibilities. Like the newborn child who must be nourished at his mother's breast in order to become healthy, the Mystical Deep Ecology society of the future must be nourished by the female perception of reality. It is thus viewed as natural and not problematic that women's opinions are given greater weight than men's. As Jones's Gaia-centric, matrifocal future scenario puts it, "Women are co-equal with men politically, although women possess absolute veto power" (Jones 1989, 235). Positions of power in the Mystical Deep Ecologist future society are thus shared cooperatively; however, one woman's opinion is enough to overrule any number of men.

Nonviolence in the Mystical Deep Ecology eutopia. The matrifocal culture of the Mystical Deep Ecology future eutopia stresses compassion toward all life and thus is remarkably peaceful. This peacefulness is structurally maintained, in part due to intermarriage and the resulting dispersal of male relatives among the villages of the immediate area. Making war on neighboring villages in this future society amounts to literally killing one's own brother. The religious-metaphysical stance of nonviolence toward the natural world inherent in Gaianism further promotes a nonviolent orientation toward the social realm.[20] The Mystical Deep Ecology eutopia is the only Green future that does not legitimate the killing of animals as right, good, and just.[21] The line of reasoning is as follows. In order to limit social violence, one must limit the entire consciousness surrounding violence wherever it occurs. This includes violence directed toward nonhuman nature. Gaian biocentricity maintains that respect for nonhuman otherness will transfer into respect for human otherness as well. Since all beings are components of the Goddess, violence is seen as the ultimate sin, a direct blow against the Goddess herself.

Mystical Deep Ecology's future eutopia contains no soldiers, hunters, or weapons. Values associated with males (aggression, anger, jealousy, and intolerance) are kept strictly in check in this future, while values associated with the feminine (cooperation, sharing, and acceptance) are encouraged and rewarded. Each young male is appointed a female mentor at birth to help achieve this harmony. Males are oriented toward fulfilling the caring and nurturing roles of housekeeper, cook, gardener, social worker, and child provider. Aggressive sports are outlawed. Games are cooperative rather than competitive. There are no losers and everyone wins. Respect for life and nonviolence are taught to each child as primary rules of life and reinforced through daily rituals and routines as simple as the personal greeting, "May peace be with you."

THE SOCIAL ECOLOGIST VISION OF THE FUTURE

Introduction

Social Ecologist theory maintains that only through the creation of a just and participatory society can a healthy and benign relationship to the natural world be developed.[22] Presupposing that the domination of man by man preceded the domination of nature by man, the Social Ecologist future is structured to eliminate all hierarchy and delegitimate all forms of discrimination. Every person is viewed as valuable to the community and worthy of community respect and mutual support. Social Ecologists argue that harmony can then be applied to ecological relationships.[23] Human beings, as nature rendered self-conscious, are seen as having a duty to respect and protect that which has given them life and continues to support them. This stewardship includes active assistance in furthering what Social Ecology describes as "the precepts of nature" (freedom, diversity, cooperation, interdependence, and development) (Bookchin 1982a; Maser 1988; Todd and Todd 1984).

The Social Ecology Eutopian Scenario

Kris felt something tickling his nose and opened his eyes. He brushed the resting butterfly off his face, shook the sleep from his eyes, and glanced around his plant-filled room. The sun was shining brightly through the large picture windows that took up the majority of space on the ceiling and four of the five walls surrounding Kris's waterbed.

"Dim," said Kris, and the windows automatically darkened a bit, letting Kris's eyes adjust to the brightness of the day outside. Nino, Kris's pet ferret, bounded from his cave in the corner of the room and stood up on his hind legs, staring inquisitively at the boy.

"Ok, ok," said Kris, responding to the ferret's stare. "Let there be light."

Instantly the windows lightened and the sun shone full force into the grotto-like room of the 10-year-old boy. Happily, the ferret bounced over to the waterfall, took a few sips of fresh, clean water, and swiped at a curious minnow who had swum too close to his furry little face.

"May I enter?" asked a gentle voice.

"Sure, Dad," answered the boy, who then asked his own question: "What's on the agenda today?"

"I thought I'd take a walk over to Community Garden B-7," answered Kris's father, "It's getting toward the end of the month, and our family's still got a few hours of service to fulfill. I heard the new dodo eggs from Palo Alta are ready to hatch, and we want to inoculate and incubate the chicks as soon as they do. Want to come along?"

"Sure," said Kris. "You know, I never saw such funny-looking birds before, but I still don't know what good they'll do the community."

"You never know," said the father, "It started as just a lark, but I suspect something interesting may come from those dodos."

"Maybe they taste good?" asked Kris. "One dodo egg all by itself is big enough for one of Sam Wagoner's special omelets. By the way, I've got an important meeting at town hall later this afternoon. My age cohort wants to sponsor a bioregional culture fair in the longhouse, and Kathleen Blaisdell and I got elected to make our case. If the dodos aren't ready, maybe you can help me with my arguments while we work on the new permaculture acre."

"Sounds good to me," answered Kris's father. "I saw Sam working on breakfast duty this morning, why don't you grab a bite to eat and bend his ear a little? Sam represented us at the Centralia bioregional gathering last year, and he might have some good ideas. Meet you later out on B-7."

Kris jumped into his coveralls, combed his light purple, blonde, and orange hair, signed out for one of the community-owned bicycles parked in the shelter a few dozen meters from his house, and followed the slim path toward town. The scenery on both sides of the path was pleasant. It was designed to be. The lightly forested hills with large grassy meadows were efficient as well as pleasing to the eye. Fruit trees and berry bushes dotted both sides of the bikeway. Abundant semidomesticated animals roamed freely around the forested pastures. Myriad small ponds, useful for a cooling swim on the warm days of summer, provided water for the animals, nesting places for a variety of edible and useful insect-eating birds, and fish for the community dining table. These ponds, the forests, and all the surrounding land belonged to no one and to everyone. They were community owned and operated. If one wished to undertake a project affecting a certain piece of land, one appealed to the appropriate committee, just as Kris was soon to do concerning his age cohort's use of the community longhouse.

Membership on such committees was a community duty, like work in the kitchen or garden or any other designated duty areas. Members were chosen at random from the community list of all citizens over 5 years old. Each committee member had an equal vote and served a one-year term. Committee decisions were overseen by the community as a whole, which could overturn any committee decision by a two-thirds vote of the citizens. Since the random selection process usually provided a sufficient overview of community opinions, this hardly ever happened. Kris remembered with glee the year the community purchasing committee was comprised primarily of citizens ranging from 13 to 20 years old. For a while there was a lot of community concern, but soon most of the citizens agreed the youth-oriented choices were good for the town as a whole.

Kris rode up to the picnic benches in front of the community dining facility. A heated exchange was taking place between a small group of neighbors at one end of the bench.

"We've got a lot of communicative action going on today from the Bioshelter Flora and Fauna Committee," said Kris.

Sam, who was sitting cross-legged under a large peach-apple tree peeling potatoes, laughed and shrugged. "Ya, they're debating whether to trade the new plum-cherry plant hybrid to Oceania for their low fat lamb gene technology. Carla says she's happy with the woolly pigs we've already got. They are lean and make much better coats than lamb's wool. And Robin has her eye on the new Oceanic solar motor for bikes and boats."

"Ya, like she doesn't need the exercise," snickered Kris. "How about trading for an automatic potato peeler as well?"

"Nah," said Sam. "If I wanted, I'd just throw them in the solar steam-peeler, but I like to take pride in my work, know what I mean?"

They both laughed. Then Kris got down to business. Despite his interest in peeling potatoes, or perhaps because of it, Sam had been a guest of several of the communities of New Columbia and beyond. Sam filled Kris with tales of community diversity and widespread differences in bioregional priority as well as with fresh eggs and hash browns. Sam suggested that Kris invite his age cohorts of the Spiritualistic Oregonians, the highly craft-oriented Hanish, and the desert community of New Pueblo to his age cohort's bioregional culture fair. Kris was familiar with these communes. Travelers who stopped by New Columbia had sometimes been from these collectives. The computer net also kept one informed, of course. But Kris had never before had reason to personally meet his age cohorts from the other collectives. He was very excited by his talk with Sam. He quickly washed and dried the dishes he had soiled and rushed off to Permaculture field B-7 to tell his Dad the news.

Analysis of the Social Ecologist Eutopia

Ecological harmony in the Social Ecologist eutopia. Unlike the Deep Ecologist futures, which advocate limited human intervention in the ecosystem, the Social Ecologist future eutopia is one where the environment is actively "improved" through consciously abetting what Social Ecology posits as "the thrust of natural evolution." This thrust consists of movement toward a more diversified, varied, and fecund biosphere (Bookchin 1982a, 342-44). The activ- ist stance of Social Ecology's eutopia calls for the integration of nature into society through the development of eco-communities and eco-technologies. These communities and technologies model themselves upon recognized pre- cepts derived from observation of the interaction between nonhuman nature and the ecosystem (Todd and Todd 1984).

The first step in the direction of furthering ecological harmony by early Social Ecologist eutopian communities was the elimination of capitalism, with its progrowth concept of progress and the resulting commodification of the natural world. Community-oriented production and local technologies based upon renewable resources and the natural limits of the bioregion were encour- aged, as was bioregional self-sufficiency. Products not produced or consumed locally were heavily taxed and used to subsidize investment in community- owned and community-managed ecological restoration projects. Factory farm- ing was slowly replaced by community permaculture gardens and aquaculture ponds. These projects were designed not only to provide food but to yield a more fertile and beautiful environment than they began with. Fruit trees were planted on every city block. Small streams were brought out of the sewers to the surface and stocked with edible fish. Wild habitats such as marshes, wilderness corridors, and small lakes were created within the community and stocked with wild animals. Eventually, the ecological restoration of the Social Ecologists was so successful it was impossible to distinguish a border between inner city and country suburbs.[24]

Social Ecology's eutopia has moved into the laboratory in diverse attempts to better nature. Genetic engineering has made plants and animals stronger, meaning more adaptable, more resistant to pests and disease, and higher yield- ing. New hybrids of plants and animals are developed yearly. Advances like the woolly swine, which provides silky wool for cloth and very lean pork, are highly valued. Some of these developments seem rather trivial, such as the plum-cherry plant, but the Social Ecologists who developed them maintain that each one adds to the diversity and fecundity of the "natural" environment. Pro- ponents of such research point to the reintroduction of extinct animals such as the dodo, passenger pigeon, and auroch as progress made toward replacement of some of the 50,000 species lost each and every year before the Social Ecolo- gist "revolution" of the year 2023 (Myers 1984, 138-39).

Social justice in the Social Ecology eutopia. Social Ecology stresses the establishment of social justice as the precondition for any kind of societal or ecological harmony to occur. Emphasis is placed upon the elimination of hier- archy and structural and personal forms of domination. The expansion of com- municative action and acceptance of communal responsibility is a further pri- ority. One of the main goals of the Social Ecologist future was the elimination of disparities in wealth and power due to age, gender, race, sexual orientation, talent, and other separatist notions. Social Ecologist communities were among the first to establish affirmative action programs setting forth the rights of minorities, gays and lesbians, women, children, the handicapped, and the aged. The values of social diversity, respect for others, nonviolence, individual freedom of choice, and self-determination are taught in every schoolroom at every grade level. All social roles are open to all people.

The Social Ecologist eutopia further stresses social justice through the establishment of social ownership and control of community property and means of production. The wealth produced by this property reverts to the community as a whole and is distributed through minimum-income programs and communal purchasing for the needs of its members. Amassing private wealth is discouraged through steep income and inheritance taxes, and societal sharing of resources and goods not currently in use is actively encouraged.

The workplace is communalized. Since all citizens share in the benefits of the community, community duties are shared by all citizens. Duty hours are allocated by family size and ability, but everyone contributes. Individuals can choose from a wide variety of community activities to fulfill these duty requirements, from the permaculture genetic laboratories, to the community kitchen, the solar cell repair shop, or whatever meets one's interests at any particular time. Community members are encouraged to partake in a wide variety of weekly duties, thus learning new skills, interacting with a diverse selection of their neighbors, and becoming more well-rounded individuals.

Democratic participation in the Social Ecologist eutopia. The Social Ecologist eutopia is a model that strives to achieve the ideal Societas civilis or civil society.[25] Citizens engage in what Vaclav Havel has called "anti-political politics." Anti-political politics rejects the instrumentalism of Machiavellian power politics to concentrate upon ways to achieve meaningful lives of "measured care for our fellow-humans."[26] In order to actualize this ideal, Social Ecologist eutopian communities adopt the motto, "Every person shall have the opportunity to participate in every decision that has an influence upon them." This motto is taken seriously, and the Social Ecologist society is structured so that decision making rises from the bottom up rather than from the top down. Democratic structures in the Social Ecologist eutopia are based upon tried political designs and social models. These include the Greek polis, the anarchist-utopian communes of the 1800s, and New England town meetings.

A wide diversity of community committees covers every possible political issue. This includes issues in the economic realm. Production decisions are made by community committees, just like any other decision. Daily work assignments and priorities are made by the workers themselves (Rohter 1991, 103-32). Similarly, educational decision making is shared between community, teachers, and students. Strong democracy, the active participation in the decisions that affect one's life, is an essential part of each child's classroom experiences (Barber 1984).

Membership on community-issue committees is chosen by random drawing and frequently rotated. At committee meetings anyone can come forth and present opinions and concerns. Everyone is encouraged to do so. Decisions are made in an open fashion, and all those attending can vote. If the vote of the committee members themselves is more than two-thirds in disagreement with the popular vote, a rehearing of the issue can be called. Decision making is reached through consensus whenever possible. Proxies are counted for those unable to attend committee meetings; however, since the questions to be voted upon are often reformulated during the open discussions, proxies are discouraged as being of limited value. Representatives to intercommunity confederational assemblies have to subject their decisions to the consensus of the home community at all times. Community membership in these intercommunity confederations is voluntary, as is individual community compliance with confederational decisionmaking.[27]

Nonviolence in the Social Ecologist eutopia. One of the main goals of the Social Ecologist future community is the elimination of structural violence through the expansion of social justice. The delegitimation of racism, sexism, ageism, and other forms of discrimination reduces violence against minorities, women, the old, the young, and the different. Societal difference is celebrated instead of repressed, leading to a reduction of personal and structural violence and a healthier, more creative and productive society in general. Courses in peace studies and nonviolence training are institutionalized in every child's classroom. The horrors of a history of war, oppression, and exploitation are driven home to every citizen. There is no production or stockpiling of weapons and no military training in this future. Active nonviolence is the norm. Individuals feeling frustration and anger seek out inner-peace counselors. Chairpersons of community committees are trained in facilitation and the furtherance of communicative processes. Affinity education, where one often assumes the roles of those with traits other than one's own, is established.

Serious disputes between communities are decided by a mediation board. This board is appointed by the Confederation of Communities, with board membership approved by the parties directly involved. Failure to abide by the mediation decision makes a community subject to total boycott—in essence, confederational shunning of the community as a whole.

SUMMARY

This chapter has illustrated what life in the future might be like should each of the three subcultures of the American Green movement be able to create their preferred eutopian society. These eutopias were assessed according to criteria established by the Greens themselves: ecological harmony, social justice, democratic participation, and nonviolence. Neo-Primitivism ranks highly for its ecological lifestyle of nomadic hunting and gathering. Mystical Deep Ecology is the only Green subculture whose cosmological underpinnings actively discourage violence toward animals. Social Ecology is strong in its support of social justice and democratic participation.

NOTES

1. This description of utopia is from Wendell Bell's *The Foundations of the Future's Field* (draft copy). Bell's chapter 6 contains an in-depth discussion of the utopian concept and the futures field.

2. See table 4 in appendix A for evidence of the widespread power of the Green vision.

3. James Dator, "Neither There nor Then: A Eutopian Alternative to the 'Development' Model of Future Society," *Human Futures*, ed. Eleonora Masini (London: IPC Science and Technology Press, 1974). In the field of utopian studies, Lyman Sargent's *British and American Utopian Literature 1516-1974* (New York: Garland, 1988) has set the standard definitions of utopia as the genre, eutopia as a good place, and dystopia as a place worse than the present. Dator adds the criteria that eutopias are feasible, motivating images.

4. Ian Wilson's "Scenarios," *The Procedures of Futures Research*, ed. Jib Fowles (Westport, CT: Greenwood Press, 1978) gives a detailed history of the concept of scenario in futures research.

5. See Bill Devall and George Sessions, *Deep Ecology* (Salt Lake City: Peregrine Smith Books, 1985). *Earth First! Journal* has had particular fun with the Neo-Primitivist notion, using cartoons of cavemen as mascots and stone axes as logos.

6. Arnold Toynbee, in *Mankind and Mother Earth* (New York: Oxford University Press, 1976), has argued that such systemic collapses of civilizations are not uncommon in human history. Chris Maser, in *The Redesigned Forest* (San Pedro: R and E Miles, 1988), believes the downfall of ancient Greek civilization was due in large part to environmental exploitation.

7. The journal *Live Wild or Die* has used the slogan, "Factories Don't Burn Themselves Down They Need Help from You!" for instance. Almost any issue of *Overthrow* or *Earth First! Journal* offers further examples.

8. See William Glasser, *The Identity Society* (New York: Harper & Row, 1975). Paul Shepard's ideas support Glasser's view of the identity society and cite the rise of war, ecological devastation, and instrumental manipulation of the earth and other human beings with the rise of agricultural society (Shepard, *The Tender Carnivore* [New York: Scribner's, 1973], 260-68). Shepard's preferred model for the Neo-Primitivist future eutopia is the Pleistocene Ice Ages (Shepard 1973, 260). Dave Foreman (*Confessions of an Eco-Warrior* [New York: Harmony Books, 1991], 56-58) disagrees with Shepard on this point and laments that it was the introduction of Cro-Magnon humanity in the Pleistocene period that brought about the extinction of Pleistocene megafauna. Foreman feels Paleolithic Neanderthalism is thus a better model for the Neo-Primitivist ecotopia.

Glasser has pointed out that although early human societies stressed cooperation and mutualism, there were also periods in which survival was precarious, and humanity's primary goal was survival. The same is true of the surviving ecosphere societies that Dolores LaChapelle ("Sacred Land, Sacred Sex," *Healing the Wounds*, ed. Judith Plant [Philadelphia: New Society, 1989], 155-58) and Gary Snyder ("Bioregional Perspectives," *Home!*, ed. Van Andruss, Christopher Plant, Judith Plant, and Eleanor Wright [Philadelphia: New Society, 1990]) use as modern models for the Neo-Primitive future.

William Cronon's depictions of Native American lifestyles in New England (Cronon, *Changes in the Land* [New York: Hill and Wang, 1983]) and Karen Liptak's analysis of Pacific Northwest Coast Indians (Liptak, *Indians of the Pacific Northwest* [New York: Facts on File, 1991]) illustrate that ecologically aware, nonagricultural cultures need not necessarily be survival oriented. Like Glasser's "primitive identity society," these cultures can be favorably compared to the modern world and found to be living a "good life."

9. William Cronon (1983) illustrates the harmony of New England Indians with the ecosystem they lived within by starkly contrasting the European consciousness of exploitation with the Native American worldview of "living with the land."

10. Several Neo-Primitivists cite the anarchist work of Kropotkin as a model of societal relations (Andruss, Plant, Plant, and Wright 1990, 74; Woodcock 1990, 43; Snyder 1990, 16).

11. Caroline Estes ("Consensus and Community," in Plant and Plant 1990, 94-103) offers examples of how such synchronization might work. Estes's theories rest on the concept of consensus, where each individual concerned about an issue has the right to express his or her opinion and participate in the decision-making process. The goal of consensus is to find decisions that everyone can agree with.

12. Dolores LaChapelle (1989) discusses purification ritualization. Sally Abbott ("The Origins of God in the Blood of the Lamb," in *Reweaving the World* ed. Diamond and Orenstein, [1990], 35-40), believes such ritualization limits violence toward animals but also alleviates the guilt involved in animal killing and thus enables such killing to take place.

13. The understanding of Gaia under Mystical Deep Ecology is very different from the scientific hypothesis presented by James Lovelock at Princeton in 1969. The scientific concept of Gaia that Lovelock, later joined by Lynn Margulis, postulated was a complex organism involving the cybernetic interaction of the earth's biosphere, atmosphere, oceans, and soil, an organization that created and maintained an optimal physical and chemical environment for life on the planet (James Lovelock, *Gaia* [Oxford: Oxford University Press, 1979], 11). According to Lovelock, his theory broke with scientific tradition, which held that life adapted to planetary conditions as given, and for the first time offered a scientific context for the idea that the earth was a living planet more similar to the human body than a dead piece of matter (Lovelock 1979, 152).

To the Mystical Deep Ecologists, who intuitively view the earth as the "sacred fount of all life," the concept of Gaia holds a particular attraction, although the scientism of Lovelock did not. Mystical Deep Ecology has solved this problem by essentially removing the science from its concept of Gaia, emphasizing instead the countless cultures that have viewed the earth in a religious-metaphysical way as Mother and Earth Goddess (David Oates, *Earth Rising* [Corvallis, OR: Oregon State University Press, 1989], 196-97, 204). Devall and Sessions (1985, 151) are typical of the antiscientific, Mystical Deep Ecologistic approach to Gaia, criticizing the "limited, cold, manipulative, distant from reality" scientific version of Gaia in favor of Gaia myths, which are "encompassing, intuitive, comforting, involving."

14. Many nonecofeminist Mystical Deep Ecologists concentrate on the latter two points while ignoring the first. Thus they do injustice to the full implications of the Gaianism in Mystical Deep Ecology. See Marti Kheel's "Ecofeminism and Deep Ecology" and Michael Zimmerman's "Deep Ecology and Ecofeminism" (both in Diamond and Orenstein 1990). Jim Cheney's "Ecofeminism and Deep Ecology," *Environmental Ethics* 9, no. 2 (Summer 1987) also offers more on this argument.

15. Riane Eisler, in "The Gaia Tradition and the Partnership Future" (Diamond and Orenstein 1990, 13), calls this image, "Our great Mother, the giver and creator of all."

16. For a comprehensive view of the ecological degradation caused by the modern meat-oriented diet, see John Robbins, *Diet for A New America* (Walpole, NH: Stillpoint, 1987). This book also stresses social, health, and social justice issues, and has become the New Testament of vegetarianism, joining the older bible, Peter Singer's *Animal Liberation* (New York: Avon Books, 1975). For a cutting-edge overview of the current ecofeminist position on animal liberation, see the *Feminists for Animal Rights Newsletter*, a quarterly newsletter covering recent books and emerging issues in the field.

17. See Riane Eisler, *Chalice and the Blade* (New York: Harper & Row, 1987) for a recent and popular example of a partnership society. Carol Kessler lists dozens of earlier models, some dating to the nineteenth century, in her excellent, annotated "Bibliography of Utopian Fiction by United States Women 1836-1988," *Utopian Studies* 1, no. 1 (1990), 1-58.

18. Other religions have not been outlawed but are viewed suspiciously as sects. Most traditional religions (such as Catholicism) were able to modify themselves sufficiently by stressing the feminine, egalitarian, and nonviolent aspects of their faith and downplaying their former emphasis on male deities and priests, domination, intolerance, and aggression.

19. According to the Mystical Ecofeminist perspective, women possess an "elemental power" due to their direct connection to the creation and maintenance of life; thus, they have a truer view of societal issues than men do. This connection in turn leads to an epistemological advantage inherent in women's biological makeup. Charlene Spretnak believes that because women "form people from our very flesh and blood and then nourish them from our breasts," women are "predisposed from a very early age to perceive connectedness in life are more empathetic, and they remain more aware of subtle, contextual 'data' in interpersonal contacts" (Spretnak, "Toward an Ecofeminist Spirituality," in Plant 1989, 128-29). This greater awareness is recognized by both men and women in the Mystical Deep Ecology future eutopia, and men appreciate and support the guidance they are given by their female mentors.

20. This is a probable assessment, but may not always be the case, as we will explore in chapter 5, "Dystopian Potential and American Green Movement Subcultures."

21. In part this is because I have concentrated upon the Mystical Ecofeminist aspects of this future. Many of these theorists see a connection between the exploitation of women and the exploitation of animals. See "Patriarchal Domination of Women, Nature and Animals: The Feminist-Animal Liberation Connection," by Gail Johnson, in the *Feminists for Animal Liberation Newsletter* 4, nos. 1 and 2 (Spring/Summer, no date): 1-3.

22. The Social Ecologist sees human beings as nature, but a very special manifestation of nature. As nature rendered self-conscious, the Social Ecologist believes humans have the utopian potential to rationally intervene in the ecosystem to direct evolu-

tion in an intentional, examined, and beneficial way (Murray Bookchin *Remaking Society* [New York: Black Rose Books, 1989], 203-4).

23. Social Ecology argues that the synthesis of social freedom and complementarity with nature found in Social Ecology will lead to a new ecological instrumentalism that would transcend the present consciousness of environmental domination to bring human consciousness to the service of both humans and nature (Janet Biehl, *Rethinking Ecofeminist Politics* [Boston: South End Press, 1991], 126-27).

24. See Ira Rohter, *A Green Hawai'i* (Honolulu: Na Kane O Ka Malo Press, 1992) and Peter Berg et al., *A Green City Program* (San Francisco: Planet Books, 1989), for excellent examples of desirable and possible Green ecocommunity visions.

25. Manfred Henningsen, "Democracy or the Promise of 'Civil Society,'" in *Linking Present Decisions to Long-Range Visions*, The World Futures Studies Federation's XI World Conference Proceedings, ed. Mika Mannermaa, (1992), 195, describes the traditional European understanding of civil society "as being the congregation of free and equal citizens deliberating about the affairs of society as a whole."

26. Vaclav Havel, "Anti-Political Politics," in ed. John Keane, *Civil Society and the State*, (London/New York: Verso, 1988), 396.

27. Jim Dator's "Futuristics and the Exercise of Anticipatory Democracy in Hawaii," in *Political Science and the Study of the Future*, ed. A. Somit (Hinsdale, IL: Dryden Press, 1974a), 187-203, recommends a future-oriented, participatory democracy similar to that described in Alvin Toffler's *Future Shock* (New York: Random House, 1970), 416-30. Ira Rohter (1992, 197-241) discusses the structural design of what he calls "Citizen-based Democracy" oriented to the cultural history of the local community.

Dystopian Potential **5**

In this chapter I wish to balance the optimism of the preferred future societies of the Neo-Primitivists, Mystical Deep Ecologists, and Social Ecologists (discussed in chapter 4) with the presentation of the dystopian potential that is inherent in the writings of American Green theorists and activists. It is hoped that by illustrating this dystopian potential, methods may be found to eliminate or balance the dangerous elements in these futures and thus encourage movement toward futures that support rather than undermine the four primary values of the American Green Movement.

The question of what constitutes a dystopia is a normative issue. To address this problem I begin with Lyman Tower Sargent's standard definition of dystopia as a "bad place" or a society that is less desirable than the existing one.[1] But this definition presents a problem for our discussion. The Greens find existing society to be very undesirable in and of itself. And no doubt many in modern society would find the Green eutopian visions presented in the last chapter to correlate closely with their own visions of dystopia. To address these problems of personal preference, I have chosen the methodological approach used in the last chapter to present and analyze the desirability of Green future societies. This approach is twofold. It includes: (1) scenario creation based upon the major texts of Green subculture advocates, and (2) incasting analysis based upon the criteria that the Greens have themselves established as their goals for a good society—ecological harmony, social justice, democratic participation, and nonviolence. Each scenario presents several hours in the thoughts and actions of a person living in a possible Green dystopia. Since this is a dystopian analysis, the four primary values have been inverted to illustrate the potential ecological disharmony, social injustice, authoritarianism, and violence within the three subcultures. Table 7 in appendix A presents an overview of the results of this process.

DYSTOPIAN POTENTIAL AND NEO-PRIMITIVISM

The Neo-Primitivist Dystopian Scenario

Falcon readied herself for the ambush. This was to be her first attack on fellow human beings, and she was ready to test her strength as a warrior. She longed for the olden days of the elders' tales, when a warrior's mettle would be tested by the strongest and the fiercest animals in the forest. Now the only prey to test one's strength against were the Strangers.

Falcon remembered the words her father spoke to her: "They aren't Real People, you know. They walk on two legs, but so do birds. They have two eyes, one nose, one mouth, but the eyes are like the eyes of a scared rabbit, the nose like that of a pig, and the mouth more like that of a fish than that of a human being. To live, we must kill the bird, the rabbit, the pig, and the fish. That is nature's law. Those who kill fearlessly shall live. They shall have honor, and they are rewarded by nature and by society accordingly. Those who do not kill live in shame, like the filthy pig, like the frightened bird. In the end it is their shame that brings death to them. Nature respects power. By remaining strong and culling the weak, we are fulfilling nature's desire."

Her father's wise words brought comfort to Falcon's heart. Times had not been good lately. Drought had come again this year to the usually lush forest valley that Falcon's tribe called home. Food was scarce in the world, and Strangers would make it scarcer. This was not the first time climate changes had brought Strangers to the once lush forest watershed that Falcon's tribe now occupied. Falcon remembered the legends of how previous dry times had led her tribe, the Real People, to the valley. She remembered the mythic tales told about the heroes among her ancestors who had fought countless battles to conquer the valley and then countless more battles to keep the prize in the hands of her people. These battles had occurred many times in the past, but never before in the 14 years that made up Falcon's short life.

The elders prophesied that the new dry times were a signal that the precious food and water the valley contained would once again be desired by others. The fact that Strangers had appeared meant the prophecy was beginning to show its truth. The heroic battles were to begin again. New tales of honor would be sung, new warriors would advance in status. Legends of the fierceness of the Real People would once again be spread throughout the land, and Strangers would come this way no more. Falcon clutched her long, obsidian-tipped spear in her right hand, felt the handle of the knife blade in her left. She thanked the gods once more for this opportunity to serve nature's will, protect her people, and increase her power. Then she patiently waited for the attack to begin.

Analysis of the Neo-Primitivist Dystopian Future Scenario

Ecological disharmony in the Neo-Primitivist dystopia. Large tracts of wilderness have been restored in the Neo-Primitivist future. This has been accomplished primarily through neglect combined with some active sabotage of dams, bridges, and power stations. Small game has returned to many areas. Still, life is hard and precarious. The limited ecological knowledge and overpopulation that accompanied the collapse of industrial society resulted in overhunting, overfishing, and overforaging of what little natural resources were left. After the Great Die-Off, as the early decades of the twenty-first century are called, human population reached the basic level of ecological sustainability in nonagricultural societies. The dominant social code of the warrior and huntsperson, where one must show bravery and skill through killing, led to the extinction of the few remaining large mammals. This included those animals that were formerly domesticated, such as horses and cattle. The animals that survived were mainly small, fast propagators like rabbits, birds, and rats. All these species are now hunted for their food value.

The foraging of the Neo-Primitivist dystopian lifestyle has a limited ecological impact, although some of the less aware and more violent tribes live by ecologically ravaging one area and then moving on to the next. Life is hard and Hobbesian. Consequently, the little ecological wisdom that exists in these tribes stresses keeping population levels as low as possible. This strategy is not really a problem, since little food is available for winter storage. Winter is known as the Starving Time. The weak, the sick, and the old die during the winter. This is seen as part of the natural balance and is viewed positively because it justly keeps the population within the limits sustainable by the ecosystem.[2]

Social injustice within the Neo-Primitivist dystopia. Neo-Primitivism's emphasis on ecological diversity and respect for the biosphere offers the hope that tolerance and compassion will somehow find a way into the social sphere. Yet the current writings of many Neo-Primitivist theorists and activists make future respect for societal otherness highly suspect. The trade-off of tribalism is often a denial of the universalism of humanity. In the dystopian scenario just described, Neo-Primitivist tribes each consider themselves the Real People. Strangers are viewed with suspicion and trepidation.[3] The problem of overpopulation (in relation to the food supply), coupled with the misanthropy and biocentric egalitarianism of many of the Neo-Primitivist tribes, has led to a general devaluation of human beings who are not immediately related to one's own tribe. Many tribes consider strangers to be the human equivalent of pests and pestilence.[4] William Aiken (1984) fears that this aspect of Neo-Primitivism could lead to a complete loss of all individual rights.[5]

The naturalist ideology held by Neo-Primitivists in this dystopian scenario maintains that the strong live and the weak die.[6] This results in a strong individualism stressing self-reliance. Those not fit for survival can thus be ethically left to their own resources to fend against natural or societal forces. This survivalist emphasis has led to a concentration upon warrior values. The dystopia is dangerous for anyone who does not hold those values or excel in warrior skills. The young, old, sick, handicapped, weak, meek, and powerless are especially vulnerable in the seminomadic cultures of the Neo-Primitivist future. These social groups are forced to do the bulk of the work. The weak serve those stronger. When times are good, strangers may be sought as slaves to do the work the weak cannot do. When food is scarce, tradition has it that the strongest eat first.

Authoritarianism within the Neo-Primitivist dystopia. Participatory democracy is virtually nonexistent in the Neo-Primitivist future dystopia.[7] Instead, decisions are made by a variety of authoritarian mechanisms. Rule in some communities is by the big man/woman of the tribe. This person may be self-appointed and rule through a Machiavellian emphasis on fear and terror. Other societies have leaders who reflect the general consensus of the community. These leaders are charismatic, powerful figures to whom deference is more or less willfully given. Other leaders are put in place and supported by powerful interest groups such as the warrior class, the religious elite, or a combination of both.[8]

Given Neo-Primitivism's attraction to warrior society and the need to survive in harsh ecological conditions, authoritarian warlords seeking to expand their realm of control rise to power in some areas. These warlords engage their tribes in a semiconstant battle for power, prestige, treasure, and territory. Those who prove themselves useful to the power holders in such societies are allowed limited participation in political decision making. This participation is limited to an advisory capacity. Those without the ability to challenge the power holders have little input.

Violence within the Neo-Primitivist dystopia. The American Green movement's value of nonviolence is the one principle that seems most problematic for the Neo-Primitivist dystopia. The Neo-Primitivist emphasis on the values of warrior society and the skills of the hunter could lead to social violence, domination, manipulation, and exploitation. Although precivilizational wars were not particularly violent by modern standards of mass destruction and genocide, intertribal conflict was not uncommon. At its very worst, Neo-Primitivism could lead to a savage future of strong warriors battling one another and exploiting everyone else within their reach.

The Neo-Primitivist glorification of hunting (a violent act involving the taking of an animal's life and the eating of its flesh) is another disturbing part of its ideology. One wonders if the rubric of biocentric egalitarianism posited by the Neo-Primitivists allows for the cannibalism of human beings, especially given the absence of other large mammals to hunt and the potential food scarcity. Some observers maintain that human and animal sacrifice, abortion, and infanticide were common among the ecosystem peoples Neo-Primitivists hold up as models for their preferred future (LaChapelle 1989, 107-8). Moreover, these observers hold, the abandonment of the old, sick, and weak when they could no longer survive without community support was equally common.

This said, one may still conclude that with the low level of technology and small number of people involved in these tribal societies, the level of violence directed toward the average individual could be much less than that found in many areas of the world today, including the modern American city. Without a specific ban on societal violence, however, the Neo-Primitivist celebration of the warrior and belief in the naturalness of violence could lead to a dystopian future rivaling the worst of the "blood-and-soil" warrior cultures we have seen in this century.

DYSTOPIAN POTENTIAL AND MYSTICAL DEEP ECOLOGY

The Mystical Deep Ecology Dystopian Scenario

Little Charlene woke from her long night's sleep, stretched lazily, and opened her eyes to observe the world around her. It was still a bit dark deep in the forest where Charlene had been told to go the night before by the First Mother. It was darker still in the ancient hollow cedar where Charlene had made her bed of cedar boughs—Live cedar for the pillow, dead cedar for the bed itself. Charlene remembered she had gathered the bed the night before, leaving a strand of her own hair to replace the branches she had "borrowed" from another cedar close by.

A psalm from the Book of Starhawk ran through her head, "We are all one in the Goddess, never borrow from your sisters without repayment."

Charlene was always careful to leave a gift in repayment for what she borrowed from the earth, be it a small strip of hand-woven ribbon to replace the wood needed for winter fires or a bit of home-cooked cornbread in thanks for the food harvested from her garden or perhaps just a personal totem of thanks for the treat of some delicious summertime berries. It was not every night that Charlene slept in a hollow tree. But it was not every day that one became a woman and a Mother of the Village either. Today was the day she had prepared for. For how long? Years, it seemed. But the wait was worth it, for yesterday was the day of the first blood. Today was the day the rituals would be fulfilled. No longer would there be little Charlene, the sister, but now, the village had a new apprentice Mother, Charlene the woman.

Charlene loved being a woman. She thanked the Goddess that she was one of the lucky ones, born of the gender with the magical powers. She thought about the duties she must soon assume. The role of Mother in Charlene's village was not connected to the bearing of children; rather it was a political and spiritual position. Mothers were in charge of the care and sustenance of the village as a whole. These were powerful and demanding roles calling for responsibility, wisdom, and compassion. Which was why only women could assume them. The village Mothers were teachers, leaders, interpreters of dreams, healers of the sick, insurers of the fertility of the fields, celebrators of the everyday victories of life, and sorrow holders of everyday loss. Perhaps most important of all, Mothers were the spinners of spells, the participants in the sacred rituals that honored the Goddess Gaia and kept Charlene's village safe. These roles and many more a Mother had to fulfill.

"Men have it so easy," thought Charlene. "Plant the fields, care for the children, clean the village, cook the meals, and attend their ever-yammering gossip sessions."

Sure, some men tried to act like women, but few succeeded in their pathetic attempts. And then their primitive side really emerged. Men were full of negative emotions they just could not control: anger, jealousy, aggression, intolerance, and the inability to accept the natural state of affairs. It was no wonder that the old times when men ruled were ones of open rape and plunder, where the deepest regions of the earth itself were brutally probed and ripped open to extract the so-called resources needed by their spurious "civilizations." Such blasphemy and defamation would never be permitted now, in the most modern and civilized of times.

"When will men accept the fact that they are just not genetically able to fulfill the leadership roles culture requires of the intuitive sex?" wondered Charlene.

Charlene heard the drumming and knew it was time to emerge from the cedar's protective womb and be born again. Outside the tree, the women of her village materialized out of the forest, chanting, praying, and calling. Charlene appeared and the women encircled her. The First Mother began to read from the Book of Plant, the Text of Bass.

"Women bleed," she read as the blood flowed down Charlene's naked leg and began to fertilize the sacred earth she stood upon.

"Women bleed," chanted the women of the village.

"Women bleed for the sins of man," First Mother read, and the chorus of Mothers rejoicingly chimed, "We bleed for the sins of men."

"We bleed to replenish the blood that has been stolen from the Great Goddess, the First Mother of all life and protector of all that is right," chanted the First Mother.

The crowd chorused, "We are sacred. We bathe the earth in our blood. We give life to all we see and that which we cannot see."

"You are sacred, Charlene," said the First Mother. "You can become a woman. Do you promise to use your blood to heal the earth, to wet the dry, to feed all life?"

"I do, sacred Mother," answered Charlene.

"Then now, Charlene," said First Mother, "you are a woman."

Cheers broke out from the crowd as they rushed toward Charlene, hugging and kissing her, welcoming her to the sacred sisterhood and sharing their sacred blood of life with each other. When Charlene and the other women returned home from the forest late that afternoon, tired, elated, and red, Charlene did not return to the home of her childhood but entered the House of Apprentice Priestesses, her new home as a woman.

Analysis of the Mystical Deep Ecology Dystopian Future

Ecological disharmony in the Mystical Deep Ecologist dystopia. The nature worship of the Mystical Deep Ecologist makes a future ecological dystopia seem improbable. However, being Gaia-centric does not necessarily exclude ecological exploitation, nature manipulation, and environmental devastation when short-term survival needs encourage such actions to be taken.[9] There is strong evidence to suggest that many civilizations that worshipped nature goddesses (including the ancient Greeks, from which the name Gaia originates) decimated their forests, overgrazed their pastoral areas, and rapidly depleted the soil of their agricultural areas (Ferkiss 1993; Maser 1988, 66). This ecological disruption, in turn, contributed to a change of climatic conditions and turned the once lush lands of the Mediterranean into virtual deserts.

One can project similar dystopian ecological possibilities into a Mystical Deep Ecologist future society. The necessity of maintaining a basic agricultural society in a temperate climatic zone could put stress on even the most ecologically aware ideologies. Since the Mystical Deep Ecologist worldview discourages penetration of the earth for coal, oil, or minerals and prefers magic to technology, it is likely that the main source of fuel for cooking and for heating would be wood or animal dung. Pressure on the forested areas still remaining would be inevitable. Similarly, the metals and plastic now used for the bulk of modern artifacts would have to be replaced by plant or animal materials. Since the Mystical Deep Ecology future is based upon a conserver society scenario, the level of materialism and consumer consumption would be drastically reduced.[10] Still, basic necessities such as housing, clothing, tools, and utensils would have to be produced, thus putting further pressure on the natural surroundings. In the case of tools and clothing, for example, it is likely that at least some instrumental use of animals would be necessary.

A return to a primarily Neolithic agricultural economy offers other problems for Mystical Deep Ecology that could lead to ecological disharmony and animal exploitation. It is likely that current high-yield crop varieties, which are dependent upon petrochemical fertilizers, pesticides, and herbicides, would no longer grow well without such human maintenance. Current agricultural products are the result of over 10,000 years of human manipulation (Myers 1984, 144). It is unlikely that this manipulation could be "uncreated," even by the best mystics of the Deep Ecologists. It is possible that farms in the Mystical Deep Ecology future dystopia would produce far less yield than farms have in times of industrialized agriculture.[11] Lower yielding crops mean large areas of land surrounding Mystical Deep Ecologist settlements would have to be converted to agricultural land. Given the lack of technology, slash-and-burn farming methods would probably be common, causing further damage to forest land.

The Mystical Deep Ecologist stance on animal rights might also have to be modified. Trapping of animal pests such as rabbits and other rodents who threaten scarce crops is likely. The use of these animals for clothing, tools, and food is probable. Sheep would be raised to provide wool for clothing. Cattle would be valued for their manure, which would be used both for fertilizer and for fuel. The grazing of this livestock would require even more natural areas to be turned into pasture. Livestock grazing would also attract predators such as wolves and coyotes. It would be only a matter of time until trapping or hunting was accepted as a means to stop these predators from attacking the valuable animal resources needed by the Mystical Deep Ecologists themselves. These changes from the ecologically benign beginnings of Mystical Deep Ecology to a more instrumental and ecologically manipulative approach would require some philosophical sacrifice of extremist positions, but then, survival usually does.[12]

Social injustice in the Mystical Deep Ecologist dystopia. When one begins to explore the Green value criterion of social justice, one encounters the most problematic aspect of the Mystical Deep Ecologist future scenario. One is particularly struck by the amount of female chauvinism expressed by Mystical Deep Ecotopians, both male and female. The male conception of God currently touted is not made gender neutral or balanced by a multitude of deities in the Mystical Deep Ecologist future but is replaced by a female figure, Gaia, the Earth Mother. Men's roles in procreation and the defense of life are ignored by the Mystical Deep Ecologists, and "masculine" value orientations are always seen as negative and in opposition to the life-affirming values innate in women. It can be easily extrapolated from the writings of current theorists, such as Charlene Spretnak (1986, 1989, 1990), that the Mystical Deep Ecologist future dystopia would merely reverse the domination and hierarchy of valuation expressed by modern andropocentric society. Rather than balance or harmonize the current inequalities, this dystopia would invert them. Women would replace men as a privileged gender.[13]

The religious-metaphysical orientation that permeates all aspects of Mystical Deep Ecologist cosmology offers further problems for the issue of social justice. Bookchin (1989, 12-13) believes that the worship of any being, natural or supernatural, is always a form of self-subjugation that leads to servitude and social domination. Another problem is that groups stressing religious-metaphysical experiencing often value intuitive and personal forms of rationality over objective forms. Emphasis is upon noncritical thought and upon accepting the "proper" intuitions one receives (Biehl 1991, 104). Inevitably, leaders arise to coordinate these intuitions (Starhawk 1988, 269). Biehl (1991, 86) maintains that these leaders constitute a segment of society that holds considerable power to manipulate their merely intuitional followers.

At the most benign level, manipulation by leadership usually results in the transformation of the leadership class into an elite with power equaling privilege. In the Mystical Deep Ecologist dystopian scenario, this process of elite creation has serious social justice implications for the status of the majority of women as well as for men.[14] Certain women are chosen by the current elite of priestesses to perpetuate a class that rules every aspect of the society. Everyone else is placed under their control "in service to the Goddess." Ena Campbell (1982, 21) actually finds an inverse relationship between goddess worship and high secular female status. Of particular interest to our dystopian scenario is the case of Minoan Crete. While many Mystical Deep Ecologists see Minoan Crete as a model of matrifocal society, Biehl (1991) sees a society where a hierarchy of priestess-controlled corporations helped to develop an extremely exploitative and oppressive civilization.[15] In our dystopian scenario, a similar hierarchy has arisen.

Authoritarianism in the Mystical Deep Ecologist dystopia. Traditional feminist perspectives refute sexist ideologies that link the oppression of women to biological rather than social factors. Many Mystical Ecofeminists reject this stance and take an essentialist position that celebrates the stereotypes of "women's nature" as innate and essentially superior.[16] The arguments that have been used historically to subjugate women (that they are biologically more caring, nurturing, emotional, and irrational) have been accepted by many Mystical Deep Ecologists and co-opted by them to function as a kind of ideological jujitsu that places women in a position far above that of men. Men are seen from this perspective as biologically aggressive, illogical, and death oriented (and thus incapable of rational thought) (Spretnak 1986, 50-51, and 1989, 129). The result of this ideology in the Mystical Deep Ecologist dystopia is that most men are treated no better than slaves or Indian untouchables by women in power. Participation by men in any form of political process is denied. The establishment of strictly controlled religious hierarchies has created a situation that is not much different for the majority of women. The emphasis on a goddess-worshipping religious-metaphysical epistemology has allowed a hierarchy of priestesses to control all major decision making in society.

Violence and the Mystical Deep Ecologist dystopia. The dystopian elements discussed in the previous three sections make suspect the nonviolent aspects of the Mystical Deep Ecology future dystopia. Privilege of one gender (or class) over another, especially when accompanied by the irrational elements of mysticism, can create a form of structural violence when one of the primary goals of the society is egalitarianism. Such privilege limits the development of both genders and suppresses the creative resources that society needs to meet the stresses of the future. Without an analysis of the social factors involved in gender stereotyping and an ethics stressing social justice and the democratic participation of all members of society, the Mystical Deep Ecology future contains the potential of dystopian oppression. Such oppression would likely lead to a frustrated and violent society.[17] As the old peace movement slogan states, "There can be no peace without justice."

The archeological evidence cited by Mystical Deep Ecologists that goddess-worshipping societies were peaceful and nonviolent is also questionable. Gimbutas (1982a, 297) has found evidence of ritualistic child sacrifice, apparently to the Mother Goddess, in several Neolithic grave sites. Peter Warren (1984, 48-54) found similar evidence, including the possibility of ritualistic cannibalism, in priestess-oriented, goddess-worshipping Minoan Crete. Other matrifocal societies, such as the Iroquois Confederation, conducted expansionist wars and were notoriously violent as warriors (Biehl 1991, 48). Mystical Deep Ecologists have ignored these violent tendencies in the societies that they put forth as future models. Thus they offer no attempt to eliminate such tendencies. By ignoring the violent dystopian potential that could exist within the Mystical Deep Ecologist future, proponents of this future are leaving themselves open to the charge that the violent inclinations seen in the past would be recreated in this future.

DYSTOPIAN POTENTIAL AND SOCIAL ECOLOGY

The Social Ecologist Dystopian Scenario

Murray looked at the duty roster even though he knew what was written on the schedule. After all, the job schedule was made a year in advance. Such advance scheduling worked well in every aspect of the colony. Unexpected events such as death and illness were easily covered by the relief crews and "voluntary" extra duty. Murray hoped that by some miracle the roster would suddenly have changed and instead of Flesh Production Warehouse Number Three being neatly printed next to his name, there would be something (anything) else. It was not that he minded the work; it was just that it was soooooo boring, month after month. The Scheduling Committee had decided four years ago that job switching was inefficient at intervals of less than six months. Murray still had two months to go on the "flesh farm" and was already weary of processing, feeding, and guarding Chicken Little.[18]

Flesh production was a serious duty. Indeed, the meat production from the biogenetically engineered, big-as-a-house masses of living flesh known (affectionately?) as Chicken Little, Big Beef, and Porky was assigned only to the most responsible of citizens. Now that these food sources had been perfected, the meat produced by these three living, but not feeling, entities fed the entire colony. And of course Chicken Little must not only be harvested for the colony to eat, but it had to be maintained as well. To keep alive a one-ton-plus mass of flesh that has no brain and very little in the way of internal organs is not a task for the irresponsible. The numerous probes stuck into the mass of Chicken Little had to be monitored for circulation and health. The climate of the warehouse had to be kept perfect as to temperature, air flow, and amount of oxygen. And of course Chicken Little had to be fed.

Chicken Little was fed a continuous diet of high-protein liquid pumped directly into its "stomach." Vitamins, minerals, amino acids, and the other essentials of healthy flesh production had to be mixed into a nutritious and properly constituted soup. Or Chicken Little would take ill. And flesh production would drop. And the colony would suffer. And since the consistency of the soup was his duty, Murray would be held responsible. Failing in one's responsibilities was not met with kindness by the communal leadership. Public explanation and self-criticism was expected. Although some of the more political of Murray's comrades enjoyed these spectacles, Murray did not. These communal sessions often turned ugly as some sought to shift blame upon others. To be a scapegoat was never a pleasant alternative, and even less so now that a particularly cruel and vindictive gang had managed to manipulate their way into many positions of communal power.

Murray yearned for a change of routine. It wasn't that he would try to shirk his responsibility to the community. Murray could hardly even imagine such a thing. After all, school lessons from kindergarten on had taught him that the sacrifice of the one for the good of the many was not really a sacrifice but a privilege. It's just that he had imagined that after six months of feeding Big Beef, the job change the Scheduling Committee would give him would be something a little different from another six months of feeding Chicken Little. The switch from one flesh production warehouse to the other was not so different, even though, as the committee had pointed out, the makeup of the feed for Chicken Little did contain less iron, more vitamin K, and a completely different mixture of steroids than that for Big Beef.

"Perhaps if I speak out more and support the Leader at the gun control meeting on Thursday, I'd get a different job," Murray thought. The commune's current Leader wished to trade scarce resources to other communes in order to stockpile even more weapons than the commune currently had.

"I really think we've got more than enough weapons already, but perhaps I don't fully understand the Leader's position," thought Murray. "After all, the Leader has the overview. He's the expert. I've been keeping so busy with my job requirements and communal duties, I haven't really had time to devote much thought to the nuances of the issue."

"Besides," Murray told himself, "if the Leader's gang wants guns, they'll get guns—one way or another. I might as well be on the winning side, for a change."

Analysis of the Social Ecologist Dystopian Future

Ecological disharmony in the Social Ecologist dystopia. The Social Ecologist future dystopia falls short of the ideal Green approach to nature in one major respect: the lack of limitation on the instrumental manipulation of nature. Social Ecologists make the point that humans must intervene in the natural world, because in fact we have no choice. The choice human beings do have, according to Social Ecology, is to make our interaction with nonhuman nature as rational as possible in meeting nonhuman and human needs (Biehl 1991, 26).

The basic flaw of this rationalist orientation, in relationship to ecological disharmony, is that Social Ecology equates the concept of human self-interest with that of ecological service to nature. Social Ecology thus posits that what is good for humanity is ipso facto good for nature as a whole. Social Ecology can advocate such a humanistic and activist viewpoint toward nature manipulation because it views human beings as nature rendered self-conscious and thus capable of recognizing and furthering the basic precepts of nature. Bookchin (1982a, 342) has gone so far as to call the ability of humans to make nature more fecund, varied, whole, and integrated the hidden desideratum of natural evolution. Given this call, it is not hard to imagine a future Social Ecologist society that is even more oriented toward the manipulation of nature than is our present society.

It is this emphasis on ecological manipulation that gives rise to the possibility of Chicken Little, Big Beef, and Porky in the future dystopian scenario. Although some Social Ecologists might view a brainless, unfeeling mass of flesh the ultimate achievement in humanistic (animal-rights-sensitive) meat production, it is unlikely that the majority of Greens would agree that this fits their ideal definition of ecological harmony.[19]

The Social Ecologist future dystopia is one where the philosophy of beneficial manipulation has gotten out of hand. The view of an ecologically rational human society has slammed into the reality of limited human knowledge of the natural world and its complex interactions. This limited knowledge base, coupled with human fallibility, has often led to unexpected, unpredictable, and negative consequences. Worst-case scenarios of the accidental escape of genetically engineered catastrophes such as artificial diseases, oil- and plastic-eating bacteria, and modified plants and animals seem to be daily occurrences. Attempts to beautify and rationalize wilderness areas have backfired, with indigenous plants being subsumed by ruthless introduced competitors and the extinction of countless plant and animal species. In essence, most of the Social Ecologist attempts to solve the problems of the postindustrial age by technological means have only created more problems and increased ecological disharmony.

Social injustice in the Social Ecologist dystopia. Social Ecologists take a dark view of the history of humanity, seeing a past where emphasis on self-interest, exploitation, greed, and violence has ruled. They also believe that human beings are naturally loving, nurturing, and social. Social Ecologists explain the disparity between the two realities by stressing the exploitation and oppression that hierarchy and scarcity force upon a society. In the Social Ecologist view, hierarchy and scarcity are linked, and this linkage leads directly to dysfunctional cultural systems. The Social Ecologist attempts to rationally create the perfect society by eliminating both scarcity and hierarchy.

In the dystopia just described, the Social Ecologist project to create the good society has become pathological. The emphasis on social manipulation and behavioralism approaches Skinnerian proportions. The Social Ecologist dystopia attempts to overcome the faults of humanity by enforcing strict ethical systems of cultural and structural restraint on unwanted social behavior. Likewise, systems of reward have been established for desired activity. Freedom, one of the most cherished values in Social Ecologist rhetoric, has essentially become the freedom to agree with community values and abide by community standards. Political correctness, meaning adherence to community norms, is valued above individualistic behavior. Required classes in "right thinking" are a lifelong institution. Attempts to avoid this conformity are viewed as dangerous to the community and as something undertaken only by the mentally ill or the criminal.

Materialism is viewed as suspect in this future. The power once wielded by the wealthy has now shifted to those who can walk the party line. Those who enjoy aggressive politics, the give and take of public debate, and the victory of winning seemingly insignificant points are especially rewarded as long as they keep within the bounds of safe discourse. Since every aspect of life in this future is viewed as political, the women and men who shape the new orthodoxy control a great deal of power.

Authoritarianism in the Social Ecologist dystopia. Politics in the Social Ecologist future dystopia has become the art of manipulation in the Machiavellian sense of power grabbing and power holding. The art of mass manipulation is highly respected among the elite, and individual manipulation is ever present in their dealings with each other. The structures and traditions of democratic participation are still in existence. Town meetings are held, but those individuals whose views are deemed reactionary, counterrevolutionary, and otherwise dissident are shouted down, ridiculed, or shut up by parliamentary procedures. Politics has become murky and unfathomable to the average citizen, whose main interest is keeping to the politically correct rather than voicing independent opinion. Subtle threats and the example of what happens to dissidents make the common citizen look for clues from the power elites as to the right way to vote. Political elites comprise the community committees, frame the political issues, choose the wording and candidates on public ballots, and control the dispersal of the resources of the community.

Violence in the Social Ecologist dystopia. The majority of physical violence in the Social Ecologist dystopia would be eliminated; however, structural violence and mental abuse would be used to enforce conformity. Self-criticism sessions such as those utilized by communist cells would be common events. Neighbors and colleagues would gladly volunteer their observations to community authorities as to how well one seemed to meet community goals and ideals. Shunning, taunting, public and private embarrassment, and bad work assignments would be the new forms of community violence replacing the overt physical violence of the present. Eternal reeducation classes would be the ultimate punishment for nonconformity.

Violence between Social Ecologist communities is a distinct possibility. The lack of centralized authority, the revolutionary/missionary zeal of some Social Ecologist communes, and the natural disparity in resources, talent, and wealth between communities could lead to tension, anger, and frustration. As in the world system of nation-state disorder today, communities that feel they do not have a fair share of a region's resources might raid other communities or demand payment from those communes less aggressive but better off materially. As in the religious fundamentalism of the present, fanatic Social Ecologist communities that saw themselves as ideologically pure would resent the impure influences of surrounding "less correct" communes and would sponsor destabilization campaigns against them. Social Ecologist communities need not necessarily abandon their weapons and could cite self-defense as a rationale for their community armories and mandatory military training classes.

An additional problem of violence arises for animal rights activists within the Greens when confronted with Social Ecology's instrumental use of traditional food animals. Bookchin (1982a, 1986a) views aquaculture, the raising of livestock, and hunting as new crafts in his future eutopia. Rohter (1992) also includes these elements in his future vision of a Green Hawaii. While animals are an integral part of any ecosystem, and the livestock raising advocated by the Social Ecologist varies greatly from the factory farming of today, the question must be raised, to what extent is the ultimate exploitation of other forms of being, the removal of life for one's own selfish desires, consistent with the Green value of nonviolence? This question is still being debated in all three subcultures of the American Green movement, and will no doubt be a source of contention for some time to come.

SUMMARY

This chapter explored the dystopian aspects of what life in the future might be like should the three subcultures of the American Green movement gain power in less than perfect times. Each dystopia evokes serious concerns because of its cosmological underpinnings. Potential areas of ecological disharmony, social injustice, authoritarianism, and violence are emphasized. All three subcultures were found to have deficiencies in each area.

NOTES

1. See Lyman Tower Sargent's *British and American Utopian Literature 1516-1974* (New York: Garland, 1988). Sargent's work delineates the standard definitions of eutopia as good place, utopia as the genre, and dystopia as a place worse than the present.

2. William Cronon's *Changes in the Land* (New York: Hill and Wang, 1983), discusses how New England Native Americans used minimum sustainability as a population control measure. Dave Foreman has echoed similar sentiments in an interview with Bill Devall in *Simply Living* 2, no. 12 (n.d).

3. Dave Foreman has stated his opposition to sanctuary for Central American refugees, for instance. He believes they belong in their own bioregions. See Ynestra King, "Coming of Age with the Greens," *Z Magazine* 1, no. 2 (Fall 1988): 19.

4. A common point of identity for Neo-Primitivism is the belief that the earth is overpopulated and human beings are a disease organism destroying the biospheric body. Foreman calls people "humanpox," for example, and considers himself an antibody protecting the earth ("The Green Guerrilla," *Entertainment Weekly*, March 22, 1991, 64). Foreman has further opposed aid for famine victims in Africa and has stated that AIDS is a natural way to reduce overpopulation. See Brian Tokar, "Exploring the New Ecologies," *Alternatives* 15, no. 4 (November/December 1988), 33-35.

5. William Aiken, "Ethical Issues in Agriculture," in *Earthbound*, ed. Tom Regan (New York: Random House, 1984), 269.

6. Foreman believes modern wilderness areas should have a no-rescue clause that leaves people to survive or not on their own, no matter what the circumstances. He cites Jimmy Colter, who walked naked for 150 miles through Blackfoot territory in 1808, as an example (David Foreman, *Confessions of an Eco-Warrior* [New York: Harmony Books, 1991], 66).

7. Unless one includes John Locke's concept of democracy as the freedom to leave and start your own society elsewhere. See Locke, "Second Treatise of Government," in *Communism, Fascism, and Democracy*, ed. Carl Cohen (1690; reprint, New York: Random House, 1972), 405-6. If this "right" is pursued by too many, it will be a revolt, as demonstrated in the former communist states of Eastern Europe.

8. Such scenarios seem historically probable, given the lack of sociological and political analysis in Neo-Primitivist theory. Murray Bookchin's *Remaking Society* (New York: Black Rose Books, 1989), 54-60 discusses the rise of hierarchy in tribal societies.

9. An example of such ecological extremism are the "plant concerns" sections of the U.S. Green Policy Platform. These sections suggest that a total ban on the importation of nonindigenous plants be implemented to increase the quality of life for indigenous plants. The "right" of plants to develop to their full potential is also stated. Further statements include the banning of herbicides, pesticides, and toxic agricultural chemicals and the elimination of predator control in order to keep the world "natural"

("Statement of the Strategic Policy Group on Lifeforms," *Green Letter/ Greener Times*, Special Edition, (Autumn 1989), 22.

10. James Dator's "The Futures of Cultures/Cultures of the Future," in *Perspectives in Cross-Cultural Pyschology*, ed. Anthony Marsella et al. (New York: Academic Press, 1979), identifies four primary alternative futures: Continued Growth, Collapse, Conserver Society, and Transformation. According to Christopher Jones in "Gaia Futures" (1989, 263), the conserver society scenario stresses frugality, conservation, limited social and geographic mobility, decentralization, deurbanization, deindustrialization, and decreased materialism in consumption and consumerism. For more information on this scenario, see the government of Canada's conception of what a conserver society might look like in Kimon Valaskakis ed., *The Conserver Society* (New York: Harper & Row, 1979).

11. Ira Rohter's *A Green Hawai'i* (Honolulu: Na Kane O Ka Malo Press, 1992), 345-47 offers arguments that "regenerative" agriculture will work without industrial support and produce higher yields than present methods. The scenario presented in this chapter is a worst case dystopia.

12. Such changes in Mystical Deep Ecology's philosophical stances would not be out of line with the views of many current Mystical Deep Ecologist theorists. Timothy Luke argues that the rituals of Deep Ecology can be seen as attempts to exert control over and manipulate the natural environment in "Deep Ecology and Distributive Justice" (Paper presented to the annual meeting of the Midwest Political Science Association, 1987), 17-18. And despite its biocentric rhetoric, Mystical Deep Ecology accepts a hierarchy of values, with human self-interest (or preference) high, if not on the top, of the list. Starhawk's "Feminist Earth-based Spirituality and Ecofeminism," in *Healing the Wounds*, ed. Plant (Philadelphia: New Society, 1989), 179-181, views the AIDS virus, diseases, and parasites that kill acid rain-weakened trees as symptoms of a declining and increasing toxic environment. "Healing" the planet, in Starhawk's sense of the word, would mean the reduction or elimination of these life forms, thus showing a discriminatory preference in terms of biocentric equality. I have no doubts that this preference would be expanded in times of extreme stress.

13. Michael Zimmerman's "Deep Ecology and Ecofeminism," in *Reweaving the World*, ed. Diamond and Orenstein (San Francisco: Sierra Club Books, 1990), 143, states that "some ecofeminists even speak as if men were so flawed that only women can solve the environmental crisis." See Charlene Spretnak's *The Spiritual Dimension of Green Politics* (Santa Fe: Bear, 1986), 30-31, and "Toward an Ecofeminist Spirituality" (in Plant 1989, 127-29), for classic examples of this reverse chauvinism. The religious-metaphysical emphasis on matrifocal spirituality that permeates every aspect of Mystical Deep Ecologist cosmology also presents significant ontological and epistemological problems for the creation of a just society. To the Mystical Deep Ecologist, the Goddess is immanent—She is inherent in every form of Being (Jones 1989, 239). Although the Goddess is immanent in all forms of Being, She is not necessarily actualized in all forms. Those forms of Being and patterns of behavior illustrating closeness to the Goddess, femininity, and nature are highly prized. The andropocentric culture of the present thus gives way to a matricentric future where feminine is "good" and masculine is "bad."

14. Marina Warner, in *Alone of All Her Sex* (New York: Knopf, 1976), 283, argues that there is no logical equivalence in any society between exalted objects of female worship and a high position for women in general.

15. See Riane Eisler's "The Gaia Tradition and the Partnership Future" (in Diamond and Orenstein 1990), 29-30, for the positive view of Minoan Crete, and Janet Biehl's *Rethinking Ecofeminist Politics* (Boston: South End Press, 1991), 39, for the negative view. It is interesting to note that the word "hierarchy" itself is etymologically derived from the Greek word for priest/priestess (Biehl 1991, 49).

16. See Zimmerman (1990, 142-43) and Biehl (1991, 9-11) for discussion of the essentialist position.

17. Janet Biehl cites several examples of social oppression related to violence in matrifocal, goddess-worshipping, nature-oriented cultures. See Biehl (1991, 32-33, 38, 48-49).

18. Chicken Little is adapted from a similar creature of the same name in Frederik Pohl and C. M. Kornbluth, *The Space Merchants* (New York: Ballantine Books, 1978).

19. Given that some instrumental activity toward the nonhuman world is necessary, the ecological question now becomes one of limitation. The Green value criterion of ecological wisdom would seem to suggest that given humankind's limited knowledge of the natural world and its processes, manipulation of nature should be limited to as great an extent as possible. According to the Worldwatch Institute, it was well-intentioned human intervention that created many of the ecological disasters we face today. Irrigation to make land more useful is a good example. Salinization of crop land due to irrigation has become a major global problem. In the United States 25 to 30 percent of irrigated land now offers lowered yields, and salt reduces the yields of an estimated 24 percent of all land irrigated globally. Eventually much of this land will become salt desert. Water tables are also dropping at dramatic rates as outflow exceeds inflow. The most vivid case is the Aral Sea, once the world's fourth largest freshwater lake, which has lost 40 percent of its surface area and 66 percent of its volume since 1960 due to irrigation outflow. Salinity has tripled and native fish species have disappeared, destroying a once thriving fishing industry. Winds pick up 43 million tons of dried salt from the exposed seabed annually and dump it on surrounding farmland, damaging harvests (Sandra Postel, "Saving Water for Agriculture," in *State of World 1990*, ed. Lester Brown [New York: Norton, 1990], 44-46). Yet Social Ecology argues just the opposite, that human beings know enough to actively and purposefully manipulate the environment in a way that is beneficial not only to humans but to the ecosystem as well. The issues of limited human knowledge, fallibility, and unexpected consequences are seldom addressed by the activist Social Ecologist, just as they are ignored by modern industrialists.

The Future of the
American Green Movement **6**

As shown in the previous chapters, the American Green movement is a complex and diverse social phenomenon. The many facets exposed when exploring the deep cosmological underpinnings of the three subcultures send forth a prismatic explosion in the light of analysis. Wonderful eutopian possibilities for the future coexist along with dangerous tendencies toward dystopia. The Greens have articulated a high set of standards for themselves (and the rest of society). How close do they actually come to realizing these goals? Would a society where the Greens had more power be better or worse than the present?

The question of the future of the Green movement itself (and each of the subcultures within it) is also significant. As posited earlier, it is likely that Green consciousness will gain more followers in the future. Many of these followers will be action oriented and attempt to change society through the incredibly diverse number of praxis orientations that abound in the three subcultures. These social change strategies range from meditation to active ecotage and have serious implications for the future of society at large.

WHERE THE GREENS STAND

The Greens and Ecological Harmony

Neo-Primitivism could be considered the most ecologically harmonious of the three subcultures, given its love of wilderness and all things wild. This love of the wild extends to the virtual rejection of domestication and thus limits instrumental manipulation to the point where even agriculture is disparaged. If one adopts a definition of ecological harmony that concentrates upon noninterference with nature, then the Neo-Primitivists can be rated very highly.

Social Ecologists dispute noninterference as the definition of ecological harmony. Instead, Social Ecology argues that people have always manipulated their environment and always will. Social Ecology advocates an active and purposeful manipulation of the natural world as progress toward an ecologically sensitive society. Social Ecologists believe that all the world is impelled toward development and that human beings have a duty to help further the potential inherent in nature (Biehl 1991; Bookchin 1982a). This duty includes the betterment of the human condition through pest control and the genetic improvement of food stocks, but it also includes increasing the fecundity and diversity of nature. Many Greens fear that this line of reasoning will lead to a future somewhat like the Social Ecologist dystopia explored in our last chapter, and demand strict limitations on human manipulation of the biosphere.[1]

Mystical Deep Ecology takes a centrist position in this instance. Mystical Deep Ecology's adoption of earthly immanence and biocentric egalitarianism places limitations on human manipulation of nature. Still, Mystical Deep Ecologists realize that human beings have certain needs and usually place these needs above those of other species. By further adding the criterion of compassionate intervention, Mystical Deep Ecologists promote human interference with nature in order to "heal" the planet or to shorten suffering.[2]

The American Green movement has no standard interpretation of ecological harmony that is set in stone. It is thus impossible to say which is the "Greenest" position. Acceptance of a nonmanipulative interpretation of ecological harmony implies that the subculture with the lowest ecological impact— Neo-Primitivism followed by Mystical Deep Ecology and finally Social Ecology—would be the "Greenest." The total rejection of technological civilization, however, may prove too high a price to pay for most modern individuals. The technological age has brought its share of problems and ecological destruction, but modern manipulation of nature has many advantages as well. The Social Ecologist argument that it is not science or technology per se that is the problem but rather the current values guiding these institutions is a strong one. Perhaps one goal of future Green consciousness might be to spawn an ecologically sensitive science focused on natural processes and an intense awareness of human fallibility. This could lead to a restrained, but not abandoned, recognition of the human need to manipulate the environment. A more subdued and humble Social Ecology or a more technologically empowered Neo-Primitivism would seem to be best bet for this goal, although one should not discount the possibility of an "enchanted science" of Mystical Deep Ecology arising.[3]

The Green Relationship to Social Justice and Democracy

The issues of social justice and democracy are so interrelated that both are addressed in this section. The ambiguity that exists in the analysis of ecological harmony (which subculture offers the best version?) is diminished when approaching the value criteria of social justice and democratic participation. The primary concerns of Social Ecology are the political and social realms—to a much greater extent than either of the deep ecologist subcultures. While Mystical Ecofeminism does present a critique of andropocentrism, Social Ecology goes so far as to argue that social justice and democracy are necessary preconditions for a society that wishes to actualize ecological harmony and/or nonviolence. To further their understanding of these values, Social Ecologists recommend experimentation utilizing various aspects of political designs and social models from the past including the Greek polis, the anarchist-utopian communes of nineteenth-century America, and New England town meetings. In adopting these models, Social Ecology places its primary emphasis upon the elimination of social hierarchy and domination and the expansion of communicative action and communal responsibility. A further goal for Social Ecology is the elimination of the currently existing disparities in wealth and power, which perpetuate social inequality and prejudice. Ageism, sexism, racism, patriarchy, and other cultural manifestations dividing people are heavily critiqued in Social Ecologist literature. Social Ecology is by far the most obvious supporter of the value criteria of social justice and democracy in the American Green movement.

Within the two deep ecologist subcultures of the American Green movement, rankings are more difficult to make. Neo-Primitivism stresses individual freedom and self-reliance as two of its fundamental precepts; thus it offers possibilities for anarchist and libertarian communities to value the democratic process. These tendencies coupled with the Neo-Primitivist regard for biocentric egalitarianism should yield a basis for social justice. Since the posited Neo-Primitive tribes of the future would be largely nomadic (in a Paleolithic sense) and eschew the domestication of animals, large amounts of goods would be hard to transport. One could thus expect a fairly egalitarian society as far as material wealth is concerned. It should be noted that this does not suggest the elimination of status. Assuming that concepts such as basic human rights and the irreducible minimum (where each member of society is assured the basic necessities of life) were adopted, this future would be ranked rather high concerning the criterion of social justice.

The main problem with Neo-Primitivism in regards to these values is that basic concepts such as human rights are not well articulated in the literature. The Neo-Primitivist emphasis on freedom, wildness, and integration into wilderness often overshadows and seems to conflict with the social justice and democratic orientations of the larger Green movement. The more subtle aspects of social justice and democracy are often left out completely, or they must be extrapolated from misanthropic statements concerning the evils of humanity as a whole. In essence, the more social of the Green goals seem to be forgotten by the Neo-Primitivist, while the more ecological goals command an inordinate amount of attention. Without the social analysis and articulation of social rights that Social Ecology stresses, Neo-Primitivism opens itself to the prejudices of racists, sexists, and misanthropes. Coupled with the code of the warrior, Neo-

Primitivism could lead to a nightmare society of eco-fascism where self-righteous and self-appointed protectors of the earth have decided to conquer or eliminate those they see as defilers.

This problem of diametrically opposed eutopian and dystopian future possibilities also exists for Mystical Deep Ecology. Although compassion and social harmony are often stated as goals by Mystical Deep Ecologists, there is an undercurrent in the literature that speaks of "right knowledge" and "right being." The emphasis on mysticism and intuitive knowledge in this subculture removes knowledge and truth from the communicative realm and places it in the private realm. An elite inner circle of truth interpreters and knowledge validators must then arise to control and legitimate acceptable common practice and belief. Critical thinking is sacrificed, and with this sacrifice comes legitimation of the powers and ways that be, regardless of their relationship to social justice and democratic action.

The Mystical Deep Ecologist's emphasis on a culture stressing goddess worship and idealization of the feminine leads one to wonder if present patriarchal society, with all its inherent injustices, would merely be turned upside down in the future, with women as the oppressors and men as the oppressed. Since the Deep Ecologist subcultures do not emphasize social or political analysis, the critical observer is forced to extrapolate the worst as well as the most favorable possibilities. If Mystical Deep Ecologists wish to avoid comparison with fascist, authoritarian, and totalitarian societies of the past, then they should stress the social rights that all members of their societies, and all of humanity, are granted. Social Ecology presents its stand on these values in no uncertain terms. If such presentations of social and political rights appear contrary to Mystical Deep Ecology, then this issue too must be addressed. Although the possibilities for socially just and democratic future societies exist for both Mystical Deep Ecology and Neo-Primitivism, without further theoretical development of their preferred political and social realms, these subcultures must be viewed as falling short concerning the Green value criteria of social justice and democratic participation.

The Greens and Nonviolence

The final value criterion of the Green movement, nonviolence, is perhaps one that all of the three subcultures stress but still fail to maximize. The Neo-Primitivist subculture, which stresses wildness, a trait often associated with violent behavior in the modern mind, may offer one of the best examples of limiting violence. Neo-Primitivism emphasizes ritualization, purification, ecological harmony, and setting right the universal "balance" before and after any violent act is undertaken. Mystical Deep Ecology does the same. The example of pulling out a piece of one's own hair when gathering cedar boughs symbolizes acknowledgment of the pain and sacrifice that the cedar tree is making and illustrates a respect for otherness.

Mystical Deep Ecology goes even further than does Neo-Primitivism in its quest for a nonviolent culture. Mystical Deep Ecologist visions of the future contain no mention of soldiers or of weapons and depict a harmonious, agricultural society oriented around the values of peace, love, and harmony. Violent behavioral traits often associated with males, including aggression, anger, jealousy, and intolerance are kept strictly in check in the Mystical Deep Ecologist eutopia, while values and behavioral traits associated with the feminine—cooperation, conciliation, sharing, and acceptance—are encouraged and rewarded.

Social Ecology also stresses nonviolence. It offers numerous examples of limiting the structural violence of the social realm linked to poverty, racism, sexism, and hierarchy. Yet in all of these futures, unnecessary violence still exists. The Social Ecologist future includes the farming of living animals for meat as a "craft." The Neo-Primitivist future involves hunting living animals for meat and raw materials. The Mystical Deep Ecology eutopia is the only future that does not celebrate this violence against animals as right, good, and just.

Minorities in both the Social Ecologist and Mystical Deep Ecologist subcultures have critiqued violence against animals, including their use as food. These theorists often see a connection between human violence against other humans and the exploitation of the natural world. The exploitation of women and the exploitation of animals have been directly linked by several theorists in both subcultures.[4] They believe the violence inherent in the act of killing another animal establishes a consciousness of violence and exploitation, which in turn is transferred to the social realm. For these theorists, stopping societal violence or violence of human against human is not enough (Abbott 1990). These theorists argue that one must limit violence wherever it occurs.

Although all three subcultures of the American Green movement attempt to limit violence in various ways, if one accepts the arguments of the ecofeminist animal liberationist movement, major portions of each subculture fall short of the Green ideal by not actively renouncing the violence inherent in the slaughter and utilitarian use of other animals.

CAN THE AMERICAN GREENS CREATE SERIOUS POLITICAL CHANGE?

The question of whether the American Green movement can create major political change lies at the core of its future prospects. Some of the earliest and most ardent supporters of the Greens have begun to express doubts (Resenbrink 1992; Satin 1990b). Satin concludes that as currently manifested, the American Green movement is more interested in internal power struggles and arguments over dogma than in serious political change. Resenbrink comes to a similar conclusion, but is more hopeful than Satin about the possibilities of Green politics in the future.

Such charges certainly are not new to the Green movement. Nor are they unfounded. Satin's accusations spring from the 1989 Green conference called to ratify a national Green platform. Ratification did occur but at a costly price. The conference alienated many, including Resenbrink and Satin, with its divisive infighting, inflammatory rhetoric, and general disrespect for others' opinions (Satin 1990b). When reading Satin's description of the 1989 national Green conference, one is reminded of the similar platform battles and divisiveness seen at the 1968 Democratic national convention, the 1992 Republican national convention, and the 1985 and 1989 West German Green Party national conventions. At these conventions, serious differences led to equally serious losses. In the case of Die Grunen, the refusal of the 1985 convention to include a ban on animal experimentation led to the resignation of Rudolf Bahro, a key theorist and founding member (Bahro 1986). The 1989 convention led to the split of the German Greens into East and West alliances, with the resultant loss of the West German seats in the Bundestag (Poguntke 1993, 50; Rudig and Franklin 1993, 55; Wiesenthal 1993, 190).

Despite these setbacks, Satin may have been premature in his judgment of the Greens. In every instance mentioned above, the crisis was overcome. In the case of the German Greens, a solid core of Green voters provides the stability the party needs for long-term success (Rudig and Franklin 1993, 53-55). Local elections in 1993 and 1994 have actually given the Greens gains over their previous highs. Wiesenthal (1993) cites the "overstrain" of the Greens in 1985 and 1990 as due to the structural demands inherent in representing diverse constituencies on cutting-edge issues that other parties will not even discuss. At times the priorities set by these diverse constituencies are bound to clash. Jobs versus ecological well-being is one obvious example.

The structural strain seen in the case of Germany's Die Grunen is also visible in the American Green movement. The Deep Ecology/Social Ecology split represents the commitment of the Greens to both the ecology of the natural world and to the poorest and most oppressed members of society. Another structural fault line lies between the (primarily) Neo-Primitivist eco-anarchists who want limited government and the Social Ecologists who recognize that a large amount of government intervention may be necessary to solve many current ills. These strains are so great that one must expect cracks in the movement. The ability of the Greens to continue as a movement despite these setbacks offers testimony that not all Green supporters are willing to abandon the movement when their highest expectations are not immediately met. Wiesenthal's research (1993, 191-204) offers a glimmer of hope for a more Green future in this regard by concluding that if not for "the commitment and sacrifice of countless local activists" who maintain their faith in the Green alternative despite the factionalism, the constant multiplicity of conflictual issues would have destroyed the Greens completely by now (Wiesenthal 1993, 204).

In light of these problems, Resenbrink (1992, 216-220) argues that the Greens should organize as a collective "house" with a common room for their common values and separate rooms for various action orientations. These "activity rooms" would include space for direct action (demonstrations, civil disobedience), creation and perpetuation of Green alternative institutions (intentional communities, street theater groups, economic enterprises), Green media activities, and specific issue organizations (as long as they are rooted in ecological theory). What Resenbrink seeks in his proposal is a centralization of sorts, which seems impossible for the Greens to achieve. The desirability of such a structure is also in doubt. Given the current level of divisiveness between the Green subcultures, it is hard to imagine that any coalition could adequately provide the framework needed to hold itself together as a cohesive unit. These integrative attempts to put the Green movement under one roof may even be counterproductive. The Greens have lost key members, due to divisiveness, at each of the several major meetings they have held.[5] Idealistic members of the movement become frustrated, and the already frustrated members leave the movement altogether.

There are serious doubts surrounding the establishment of a Green centralized organization in the first place. As shown throughout this text, the basic precepts of the three subculture's worldviews, praxis orientations, and visions of positive futures contain significant differences. What happened in the centralization process of more established Green movements is that certain tendencies were eventually moderated or excluded completely. While certain extremist elements not consistent with the four Green values should be eliminated, when an organization "cleans house," it sometimes throws the baby out with the bath water. An example of this is the purge of the Marxists and ecological fundamentalists from the West German Die Grunen over its first ten years of life (Bahro 1986; Wiesenthal 1993, 212-13). As Green parties elsewhere have won electoral success and attempted to maintain their new positions of responsibility, they have adopted increasingly centrist positions. Those on the Green periphery, be it the cutting-edge or the leftover activists from previous noncenter movements, end up withdrawing their support (or being forced out), and issue positions are narrowed even further. This can be seen in supporters' abandonment of the New Values Party after its success in New Zealand (Rainbow 1993). Green supporters in Tasmania noted similar complaints after Green Party coalition governance there in 1989 (Hay 1992). The Greens/Green Party USA's rejection of strong positions on the issues of animal rights and marijuana legalization, despite strong support for these issues within the party, illustrates centrist tendencies at work in the American Greens. The homogenizing of these originally diverse and divisive organizations may prove to be as dangerous to the movement as a whole as those ills they seek to prevent. Centralization and institutionalization may bring power, but they also can create dogma, corruption, and a narrowing of ideals to the point where original intent is lost. The history of the Catholic Church and the Soviet Union serve as apt examples.

The successes or failures of highly centralized Green organizations or networks are viewed by some observers as worth little concern. "Greenness" is viewed by them as a state of consciousness. They celebrate its appearance in all its myriad forms. The ancient Hawaiians saw the mother goddess Haumea as having "four thousand forms and four thousand more forms, and yet thousands and thousands of forms" (Dudley, 1990, 75). Green consciousness seems to appear in a similar way. An overlaying value structure in the recognition of the four dominant value orientations can be distinguished. In this text, definite subculture derivatives of this overall consciousness have been shown to exist as well. Within these archetypal subcultures are as many individual interpretations of Greenness as there are people in the movement. To assume that some overall linkage and coordination of these diverse derivatives under one umbrella organization is possible seems to be asking for too much.

It thus seems natural to expect chaos in the Greens. If Green consciousness is to form the basis of a cosmology for the future (as it has the potential but not the inevitable possibility to do) it must manifest itself as did Haumea, in thousands and thousands of forms. It is unfortunate that some people within the movement think of themselves as having the monopoly on "Green truth." Such nonsense has no place in Green thought. Valid critique and difference, yes; dogmatism, no.

This does not mean a future where members of the various subcultures work together for common goals is unforeseeable. They do this now, in certain situations. Indeed, many members of the Greens exhibit tendencies toward more than one subculture affiliation. The strength of subculture affiliation may often be situational, changing as the circumstances and immediate environment requires. What is unlikely, however, is that a single centralized Green organization comprised of the subculture triad posited in this book will ever seriously threaten the status quo. This being said, a further caveat must be added. The threat of political change activity by coalitions within the individual subcultures themselves should not be underrated. It is very likely that the three Green subcultures explored in this text will continue to grow and have a serious impact on the future of the American political scene.

THE FUTURE AND THE SUBCULTURES OF THE AMERICAN GREEN MOVEMENT

Neo-Primitivism

The future of Neo-Primitivism will be heavily influenced by two primary factors. The first concerns the continuing trends of environmental degradation and destruction of wilderness in America. It is unlikely that we will see any drastic change in these trends, at least in the near future, due to their traditional linkage with the expansion of the economic realm. All powerful political players in America today see economic expansion as a worthwhile public policy and accept some environmental degradation as an unfortunate but inevitable result. As the negative environmental impacts associated with maintaining our technological comfort level continues to spread to populations in relatively unspoiled areas, it is likely that a certain percentage of the people in those areas will be drawn to the philosophy of Neo-Primitivism. No doubt a number of these people will be drawn to Neo-Primitivist tactics as well. Thus a future of increased active ecological resistance is virtually assured.

The second major factor shaping the future of Neo-Primitivism will be the official reaction to Neo-Primitivist activities. Presently, official reaction to active ecological resistance seems to have two goals: (1) punishing the perpetrator of the activity, and (2) limiting the expansion of such activity. The methods utilized to achieve these two goals include extensive private and government surveillance, infiltration of suspected Neo-Primitivist cells, an increase in penalties for ecodefensive activity, an increase in covert and overt negative public relations and media coverage, and a variety of counterintelligence operations similar to the FBI's COINTELPRO reaction to the antiwar and civil rights activism of the 1960s and 1970s.[6]

One consequence of the increase in legal penalties, SLAPP (strategic lawsuits against public participation) suits, and harassment of Neo-Primitivist active ecological resisters is the recognition that overt active ecological resistance can carry serious penalties.[7] This recognition may result in reducing the amount of overt active ecological resistance. Another possibility is that overt active ecological resistance will be driven underground into covert operations. To the ecodefender the covert strategy has a prime advantage in that very few covert active ecological resisters have ever been arrested and even fewer have been successfully prosecuted.[8] Ecological activists feeling the urgent need to undertake ecodefensive action may decide the small risk of getting caught while undertaking covert active ecological resistance is a more attractive option than the almost certain penalties associated with overt active ecological resistance.

Government and corporate attempts to limit Neo-Primitivist praxis may thus have the unintended side effect of increasing the activity that they find most undesirable. While overt ecological resisters are languishing in jail, struggling to raise funds for legal fees and fines, and fighting the consequences of harassment, covert ecodefenders are planning and undertaking their next actions. Surely this fact has not gone unnoticed by aware adherents of Neo-Primitivism. It thus appears likely that an increase in covert active ecological resistance is imminent in the future despite and perhaps because of increased official suppression of overt ecodefensive activity.[9]

A likely consequence of increased covert active ecological resistance in the future should be the increased formation of small Neo-Primitivist groups of ideologically similar individuals bound together in common trust with common purpose. These groups could eventually become the tribes discussed in our future scenarios in chapters 4 and 5. Earth First!, the largest and most known Neo-Primitivist network, offers a prime example of this familial, anarchistic orientation in development. The Earth First! network itself is organized into cells consisting of small groups of trusted acquaintances. The published ecodefense guidebooks encourage this structure and recommend that ecodefenders become known as ecodefenders only to those to whom they would entrust their lives (Foreman 1991, 163). A bond close to that of kinship, perhaps closer than that of modern kinship in America, is thus established and nurtured through undertaking illegal (but in Neo-Primitivist eyes, sacred) activity against common enemies. It is likely that in a future of increasing suppression of Neo-Primitivist activity, these kinship bonds and group identities will become even stronger. Many members of Earth First! already view themselves as separate from ordinary Americans. They consider themselves members of a tribe in opposition not only to American culture, but to civilization in general.

The question raised at this point is how far these eco-warriors are willing to go to achieve their goals. Humans are not presently being targeted by Neo-Primitivists. Some will argue that tree spiking represents such targeting. However, serious efforts are made to warn loggers of spiked areas and eliminate possible injury arising from these Neo-Primitivist activities. Earth First! has publicly disavowed violent action toward humans and discourages the use of explosives, firearms, and arson.

In the case of the Icelandic whaling fleet sinking, the Sea Shepherds deliberately left afloat one whaling ship due to a sleeping guard on duty. Still, it must be taken into account that monkeywrenching is a direct outgrowth of guerrilla war theory (Foreman, 1991, 162). Doug Bandow (1990), of the conservative Heritage Foundation, believes that ecodefensive actions are ecoterrorism, and foresees a day when these activities will escalate to include the murder of innocent workers and park employees. Since Neo-Primitivists view themselves as warriors and "antibodies against the cancerous disease of humankind" and spout slogans such as No compromise in defense of Mother Earth, Factories don't burn themselves down they need help from you, and Go clear-cut in Hell, one must wonder at what point ecological destruction will turn the Neo-Primitivist from anticivilizational and misanthropic rhetoric to reality. Rik Scarce (1990, 266) cites a veteran eco-warrior who states that "someday shooting timber workers would replace monkeywrenching as the most drastic means for saving old-growth trees." Sheriff Jim Weed, of Okanogan County in Washington State, has publicly associated Earth First! with a near fatal lumber mill injury, a gun battle at a lumber camp, and a fatal helicopter crash ("Smoke Weed," 1988, 24-25). None of these charges resulted in prosecution and all of the charges are denied by Earth First! Still, charges of this nature represent the very real possibilities inherent in an ideology that purports to side with the bears in a war against humanity. One wonders at what point the combination of misanthropy, apocalyptic rhetoric, and biocentric egalitarianism will lead to the rationale that the lesser of two evils involves killing a few timber company executives or road surveyors, in order to save a living ecosystem comprised of countless species vital to sustaining the biosphere in one of the last remaining virgin old-growth forests of the Pacific Northwest. Increased wilderness destruction and the suppression of overt active ecological resistance by governmental and private interests may unfortunately lead us to an answer in the near future.

The Future and Mystical Deep Ecology

The religious-metaphysical impulse has existed as long as human society itself and has been a part of every human culture. The American Green movement subculture of Mystical Deep Ecology thus taps a very ancient part of the human psyche. Even in the face of constant repression and attempted extermination, mysticism has managed to survive. In America, despite cycles of boom and bust, religious-metaphysical impulses have always had a major influence. Even in our seemingly secularized culture, over 90 percent of Americans profess a belief in God, although their interpretations of this God and their understanding of how to properly relate to the deity are fragmented into over 1,500 different religious doctrines (Woodward 1993).

While still a minor force on the American religious scene, the 20,000-plus adherents of ecological spiritualism have played a major role in the philosophy of the American Greens.[10] Time and time again, otherwise secular ecologists come to the conclusion that some sort of spiritualistic awakening related to ecological values is needed to reverse modern trends of utilitarianism and instrumentalism (Ferkiss 1993; Resenbrink 1992). Chris Jones (1989) argues that such an awakening will fundamentally challenge the basic structures of governance and economics by introducing the "new values" of respect for all life, reverence for wilderness, and respect for diversity. Many Greens see a dark side to Mystical Deep Ecology's emphasis on spirituality, however. Arne Naess (1988), who first coined the term "Deep Ecology," is quick to point out that a deeply ecological worldview needs no spiritual orientation. Naess (1988) further offers three reasons for Deep Ecologists to avoid the mystical tradition:

1. Mystical traditions stress dissolution of the individual in a nondiversified supreme whole,
2. The modern scientific community has strongly associated mysticism with vagueness and confusion, and
3. The consciousness that mystics seek is rarely sustained under normal, everyday conditions.

Most Social Ecologists readily concur with Naess. Janet Biehl (1991) and John Dryzek (1990) harshly critique the holism of Mystical Deep Ecology, with Dryzek calling it "the essence of totalitarianism." Other critiques of Mystical Deep Ecology include David Oates (1989), who believes the antiscientism inherent in Mystical Deep Ecology rejects valid scientific discovery; Sally Abbott (1990) and Tim Luke (1988), who believe Mystical Deep Ecology cloaks a crude instrumentalism that seeks to manipulate the environment while denying that manipulation; and George Bradford (1989), who sees a hidden anthropocentrism behind the biocentric rhetoric of Mystical Deep Ecologists.

The Mystical Ecofeminist derivative of Mystical Deep Ecology is a special target for Social Ecologist/Ecofeminist Janet Biehl. Biehl (1988, 1991) sees no linkage between Goddess worship and social justice and argues that religious communities are often ruled by exploitative priestly hierarchies that prey upon the superstitious fears of their followers. Biehl sees further problems in the emphasis Mystical Ecofeminists place upon myth rather than reality. The primary problem for Biehl is that the politics of myth is based upon appeal to intuition and emotion, a private realm of experience, rather than communicative and thus objective reality. Biehl critiques the Mystical Deep Ecologist stance that whatever is privately intuited, felt, or dreamed is thus as real as any other measure of reality. She maintains that mythology based upon emotive storytelling is not open to rational discussion, but is open to manipulation by unscrupulous leaders.

Rational discussion and validation of certain unorthodox intuitions is actively discouraged by some Mystical Ecofeminist leaders. Starhawk (1988, 104) is typical of this aspect of Mystical Ecofeminist praxis when she instructs her initiates to actively suppress the critical mind, saying "all you voices. . . telling us we're bad or wrong or stupid or crazy—leave right now. . . increase the power of this banishing, accompany the word with shouts, yells, footstomping." The world of rational self-doubt is thus driven away, and the new mystically based ecofeminist worldview can be accepted uncritically. The danger in such suppression of critical thinking lies in the possibility that self-doubt may exist for a valid reason.

The problem of leadership in the intuitive group is also one that should be addressed. Leaders who discourage individual critical thinking in favor of intuitive group understanding have often misused their power. Biehl has warned of such possibilities within Mystical Ecofeminism and maintains that Mystical Ecofeminist group leaders constitute "an elite with considerable power to manipulate the merely intuiting congregants" (Biehl 1991, 86). Mystical Ecofeminist leaders are aware of the power they hold, but they dismiss the negative implications of Biehl. Starhawk (1989) believes the intuitive group needs leaders because leaders are the brains of the group and the "benders and shapers of reality."

Margot Adler (1989) argues that the neopaganistic methods used by Mystical Ecofeminism are nonauthoritarian and likens Mystical Ecofeminist ceremonies to "just a gathering of friends." Adler (1989, 154) further maintains that the power over the initiate that the group leader holds during rituals is temporary and "when the drum stops and the dancing and chanting ceases, you can come back to a very grounded and rational self." While Adler may be correct in this respect, the history of semimystical political movements does not seem to warrant disregard of Biehl's warning.

Despite these critiques, it seems likely that the Mystical Deep Ecology sub-culture of the American Green movement will continue to grow and thrive. This does not mean that a Mystical Deep Ecology takeover of the Greens or any other segment of society lies in the near future but rather acknowledges the observations of Matthew Gilbert, who sees spirituality as the recognition of a fundamental truth—that the center of all things is spirit and not materiality (Gilbert 1988). Even such adamant critics as Murray Bookchin (1982a, 1989) recognize the limitations and domination of modern rationality and the need to experience basic perceptions and truths that science denies and modern society ignores. Mystical Deep Ecology fills this void and thus plays an important role in the ecology movement, a role that is unlikely to disappear. How strong Mystical Deep Ecology will grow is subject to speculation. Mystical Deep Ecology is what futurists call "a wild card." It is an unpredictable element that has the potential to radically change the future and also the potential not to. It is con-ceivable that, given the makeup and orientation of Mystical Deep Ecology and the current alienation of many with the modern world, a charismatic figure could arise and start a major religious (and political) movement. There are many minor figures in the Mystical Deep Ecology movement who are seeking such a role. None has had what it takes to expand the movement into the mainstream culture yet, but it cannot be ruled out that such an occurrence will not happen in the future. A more likely scenario is that Mystical Deep Ecology will continue to survive on the fringe of society as an essentially apolitical and private spiritual preference, while occasionally empowering its adherents to political change activity similar to that undertaken by Neo-Primitivists and So-cial Ecologists.

The Future and Social Ecology

Social Ecology has the greatest potential for political impact of all the three subcultures in the American Green movement. This potential exists, however, only in a Social Ecology that is broadly defined and carefully adapts its rhetoric to meet the hopes and dreams of the average American citizen. This should not be so difficult a task. America has a long tradition of support for egalitarian and libertarian ideals. These traditions include the abolitionist, feminist, peace, populist, and progressive movements of the nineteenth century. In the twentieth century, we have seen several of these movements rise again along with strong ecological and countermaterialist sentiments.

Despite rhetoric to the contrary, polls show that the American public is concerned about the environment. Seventy-eight percent of Americans consider themselves environmentalists (Hueber 1991). This is a larger percentage of the population than the combined total of those Americans identifying themselves as Republicans and Democrats. The history of ecological awareness and conservation in America is long and strong. Despite the wanton waste of what were seen by some as overabundant natural resources, other early Americans advocated reserving areas of forest for posterity. Official government preservation of an ecosystem for nonutilitarian purposes was achieved first in the United States in 1864 (Maser 1982, 26). The first national park in the world was established in America in 1872 (Runte 1987, 33). By 1891, Congress had created three major forest reserves (Allin 1982, 34-36). In this century the United States has often continued its ecological leadership in wilderness preservation. An executive order of Teddy Roosevelt established the first wildlife refuge in America in 1902. In more recent years, Congress has passed the Wilderness Act of 1964; the Endangered Species Acts of 1966, 1969, and 1973; and the Wild and Scenic Rivers Act of 1968. The National Parks and Recreation Act of 1978 established eight new wilderness areas totaling almost two million acres and doubling the total designated wilderness in the national park system. The Alaska National Interest Lands Conservation Act of 1980 did more for wilderness preservation than any previous law in history. More than 32 million acres were designated for wilderness preservation under the national park system, and just under 55 million acres were set aside in the national wildlife refuge system. In addition, the total wilderness acreage in the national forest system was tripled (Allin 1982).

The long history of American peace movements, workers' movements, communitarian movements, and movements for social justice and democracy discussed in chapter 2 is also the ancestor of Social Ecology. Yet Social Ecologists have not stressed these American traditions in their writings. This is a major weakness. These histories, coupled with the "grand American tradition" of seeking the good life through community service, reflection, simplicity, and self-improvement, could be used by Social Ecology to counter the currently dominant vision of success which entails the frantic rush for material and status accumulation. Radical Social Ecology makes a mistake by using the anticapitalist rhetoric of Marx rather than the agrarian communitarianism of Jefferson, the transcendentalism of Thoreau, and the nonviolent egalitarianism of Martin Luthur King. By not adopting the language of American heroes and instead favoring the rhetoric of the intellectual Left, radical Social Ecology not only fails to win over new converts from mainstream America but also manages to alienate its more reform-minded allies. The struggle over how to critique capitalism (or whether to at all) is ever present at major Green gatherings, and has been a divisive force within the movement ("The Role of Capitalism," 1989). If radical Social Ecology is to grow and prosper beyond the confines of Vermont, New York, and its other strongholds, it will have to adapt its message to one more acceptable to those it wishes to reach.

This does not mean that Social Ecologists should forsake their visions of radical political, economic, and social change. Indeed, these visions are the source of Social Ecology's strength. Bookchin's Institute for Social Ecology, the Todds' New Alchemy Institute, and projects like Detroit Summer serve as important transition points in channeling this vision into praxis. Ira Rohter's *A Green Hawai'i: Sourcebook for Development Alternatives* (1992) lists literally hundreds of ongoing community projects that fit into the Social Ecologist eutopian scenario. Rohter has taken these international examples and adapted them to his specific community, using local history, culture, and language to provide a blueprint (Greenprint?) for positive change. This is the kind of work the American Greens need more of.

The question of how to actualize the Social Ecologist vision is one that further divides the subculture. Radical Social Ecologists, primarily followers of Bookchin, believe work in local communities to be the primary route to Greening America. A newer subgroup of Social Ecology has become prominent recently by challenging this approach and advocating electoral politics through a nationwide and several statewide Green third parties. Green party activists argue that their approach can strengthen ties between the Greens and other movements, help the Greens gain legitimacy and publicity, and permit official Green input into future public policy questions (Tokar 1991). Radical Social Ecologists view the third-party approach as premature, and wasteful of scarce Green energy and resources, and as a betrayal of Bookchin's libertarian municipalization.

The fundamental question surrounding the Green parties debate concerns the extent of change available to those finding themselves inside political institutions. Radical Social Ecologists fear that successful Green candidates may find themselves in positions where holding on to power becomes more important than initiating Green change. They worry about the examples of Germany, Tasmania, and New Zealand, where Green parties have compromised and have cast away vital political positions as being too extreme (Bahro 1986; Hay 1992; Rainbow 1993; Wiesenthal 1993).

On the other hand, the success of Green Parties in Europe and the Pacific has had a major influence on the traditionally dominant parties (Rainbow 1993; Wiesenthal 1993, 202-12). In Germany the two major parties, the Christian Democratic Union and the Social Democratic Party, have adopted several Green positions, including stances reflecting greater ecological awareness and the systematic incorporation of women into positions of leadership within their parties (Poguntke 1993). The power of the Greens is felt so strongly that in February 1994, the party convention of the ruling conservative Christian Democratic Union brought forth a major battle over modifying the 45-year-old description of its policies from "social market economics" to "ecological and social market economics." The change to a more public ecological stance was eventually approved by a 359 to 277 majority ("Kohl Calls for Party Unity," 1994). With such changes toward Green stances occurring, the result of Green Party involvement in traditional politics is one of mutual co-optation. The Greens are made more moderate by the electoral system, while the traditional parties are "radicalized" by addressing issues and adopting positions they would normally avoid.

One major problem for third parties in American politics is that even successful ones have not had very long lives. In the 1880s and 1890s, the Populist
movement had organized 40,000 local alliances, elected dozens of members to
Congress, and hundreds of state legislators (Goodwyn 1976). Populism's critique of the corporate state represented millions of workers, small farmers, and
impoverished Americans, who joined the movement. By 1896, Populists had
the support of 25 to 45 percent of the electorate in at least twenty states and
came in second only to the Republicans in many states in the West and Midwest. Yet as we know, in American politics, second place is no place. Populist
politicians sought to broaden their appeal and become "fusion" candidates in
order to get and then stay elected. In the end this fusion destroyed populist
uniqueness and the radical political potential of the movement (Degler 1977;
Goodwyn 1976, 430-31).

Populist calls for radical structural change in the economic and political
systems gave way to Progressive reformism. The dreams of a Jeffersonian democracy and an agrarian society were supplanted by advocates of industrialism
and the Gilded Age. In the era of the Populists, major changes were occurring
in American society and culture. Many of these changes were outside the control of any political party of the times. In the 1880s one out of every five mid-
westerners was living in a city of 4,000 people or less; by the 1890s the figure
had changed to one out of three (Degler 1977). Although trusts were "busted,"
by 1904 three hundred industrial corporations had the power to directly influence over four fifths of all the nation's manufacturing. Economic power translated into political power and the effective negation of radical reform. By 1929
only two hundred corporations held 48 percent of all corporate assets and 58
percent of net capital assets (Trachtenberg 1982, 4). After the consolidation of
wealth that took place in America during the Reagan-Bush presidencies, the
picture does not look all that different today (Phillips 1990).

The Populist movement and later the Progressive movement, as powerful
as they were, could not stop these trends, but these movements did help to curb
their excesses. A minimum wage for women, prohibition of child labor, work-
men's compensation, and social insurance were advocated in the Progressive
platform of 1912, as were calls for referendum, recall, initiative, and campaign
finance disclosure (Link 1954, 16). It should be noted that while such demands
were made and eventually accepted, it is likely that the mass demonstrations,
strikes, and nonelectoral tactics of the larger social change movements also
involved may have had a greater effect upon public policy than did the organization of political parties (Rubenstein 1970).

Many former Populists, not happy with Progressive reformism, took a more
radical road and helped form the Socialist Party of America in 1901. By the
1912 elections, the Socialist presidential candidate, Eugene V. Debs, polled
897,000 votes, about 6 percent of the total cast. But by 1936 the Socialist Party
in America, like its predecessors, had virtually disappeared. In part the blame
for its failure lay in internal factionalism—the failure to adequately organize as

a party—and the active ignorance concerning local issues. In part, the party failed because of government repression and the reformism of Roosevelt's New Deal (Shannon 1955).

Other third parties that have attempted political change in America have had even shorter lives. The Libertarian Party, the Peace and Freedom Party, the Citizens Party, and the dozens of other little organizations that have sprung up to challenge the American political arena might better be called "fourth parties" for the slight influence they have had. More serious third-party challenges, such as Teddy Roosevelt's Bull Moose Party and the more recent attempts of George Wallace, John Anderson, and H. Ross Perot, have been onetime wonders that, at best, have played the part of spoiler rather than long-term political change agent (Ogden 1992).

There are valuable lessons for the Greens to learn from the serious study of these movements and parties. The most successful movements in American history started at the local level, with a largely dissatisfied and unrepresented public, and later organized upward (Cooney and Michalowski 1987; Flexner 1972; Rubenstein 1970). Many observers of the modern political scene believe a similar dissatisfied and underrepresented constituency exists today (Slaton 1992; Tokar 1991). If the Greens continue their focus on the local level, it is entirely possible they could combine both strategies advocated by Social Ecologists. Green parties have the potential to gain significant political influence in many communities throughout the United States. Building on this constituency could then help bring about the community confederations advocated by radical Social Ecology.

If such a scenario is to occur, the Green tendency toward divisive infighting will have to be controlled. Such infighting is now taken to extremes that serve little positive purpose. Natural allies must recognize and appreciate their differences. Some Social Ecologists will always be drawn to third-party organizing, just as others will be drawn to community activism. The success of both factions will benefit from the success of the other. Without the backing of the larger Green movement and other related special-interest movements, it highly unlikely that Green parties will be able to play an important role in electoral politics in America. Green politicians must remain true to the basic values and goals of the Green movement in order to: (1) gain the support of natural Green allies in the feminist, peace, social justice, and ecological movements and in the general population, and, (2) shift political discourse in America in a Green direction. Green electoral campaigns can bring significant amounts of attention to Green goals and values and can mobilize resources that otherwise might not be available. Despite the limitations, Green electoral campaigns thus deserve the support of all Green subcultures and related single-interest movements.

CONCLUSIONS

Each of the three subcultures of the American Green movement plays a unique and very specific role in the propagation of a new view of the world. Each of these roles appeals to certain types of people. Many of these people are not likely to gravitate toward other subcultures in the Green movement. This may not be as problematic as it seems to those seeking Green unity. In diversity there is creativity and the possibility of increased adaptation. These qualities will be needed in the changing times that the Greens will face in the future. Green dogmatists who believe they have a monopoly on "Green truth" ignore this reality and hurt the movement. While constructive criticism and warnings as to the dangers inherent in certain tendencies and philosophies are needed and should be welcomed (and heeded by subculture proponents who wish to make their subcultures even stronger), the main challenge facing the American Green movement today should be one of inclusion rather than exclusion.

This does not mean that the Greens need a centralized organization; in fact, this seems impossible given the differences in worldview, praxis orientation, and eutopian vision exhibited by the three subcultures explored in this study. What it does mean is that the Greens should recognize that despite their differences, the Green subcultures have much in common. If the Green assessment of the present state of the world is correct, then much needs to be done by as many diverse factions in as many diverse ways as possible. The sooner the American Green movement realizes this, reduces its infighting, and begins to concentrate on encouraging all of its supporters to make whatever personal or political changes they deem necessary (in the context of ecological wisdom, social justice, democratic participation, and nonviolence), the greater the likelihood the Greens have of becoming a serious and significant force for political and cultural change in America's future.

NOTES

1. Eckersley argues in "Devining Evolution" (*Environmental Ethics* 11, no. 2 [Summer 1989]: 109-66), that humankind's participation in the natural realm has been too active and perhaps humans need more humility and less activism in regards to manipulation of the natural world. She further contends that even if Social Ecology is "right" in its assessment of the telos of nature, "this discovery does not tell us why we ought to further it" (Eckersley 1989, 109).

2. "Feminist Earth-based Spirituality and Ecofeminism" by Starhawk (in *Healing the Wounds*, ed. Judith Plant [Philadelphia: New Society, 1989]), offers further examples in which human interest takes precedence over biocentric egalitarianism, and explains how compassion fits into her schemata.

3. An enchanted science would be a ritual-based manipulation of nature, in tune with certain recognized ecological precepts and shrouded with the cover of working with nature's intent rather than making nature work against its will.

4. The group Feminists for Animal Rights (Berkeley, CA) is devoted to making the connection between violence against women and animals clear. Their newsletter is full of articles and book reviews making this argument.

5. Christa Slaton and John Resenbrink are both examples of Green leaders who have quit in frustration. See "You Don't Have to Be a Baby to Cry" (*New Options*, September 24, 1990), by Mark Satin for an overview of the Boulder, Colorado, Green conference leading to their resignations.

6. See *Agents of Repression* by Ward Churchill (Boston: South End Press, 1988) for an overview of FBI COINTELPRO operations against social change activists and American dissidents.

7. See *Confessions of an Eco-Warrior* by Dave Foreman (New York: Harmony Books, 1991), 16, 124-27, and 161-63) for an overview of government and private harassment of Neo-Primitivist activists.

8. To a large degree this failure is due to the consciousness of the covert ecodefender. Covert Neo-Primitivists are out to accomplish only one goal—the prevention or delay in the destruction of a certain specified piece of wilderness. They know their actions are illegal and take every precaution to avoid detection.

9. An accounting of the extent of covert active ecological resistance is hard to come by, due to the desire of government and industry to discourage publicity surrounding this area. Using figures readily available, one can begin to glimpse the extent of ecodefense that takes place in the United States today. Jim McCauley of the Association of Oregon Loggers estimates the average cost of an ecodefensive incident in Oregon to be $60,000 (Foreman 1991; see also Chris Manes, *Green Rage* [Boston: Little, Brown, 1990a]). At this average, it can be estimated that over 300 covert ecodefense actions take place every year in national forests alone. Given an estimated membership in Earth First!, the most visible proponent of ecodefense, of 10,000 in 1989, with a core of sympathizers estimated at over 100,000 in the mainstream environmental movement, it is likely that over 1,000 acts of ecodefense take place each year (Manes 1990, 76; Mike Roselle, "Mike Roselle, Co-Founder of Earth First! on Direct Action," *Ecology Center Newsletter*, Berkeley, CA, July 1989, 3). The 1,000 incidents of ecodefense allows that many, and perhaps most, Earth First! members do not engage in active ecological resistance and recognizes that Earth First! is only one of several ecodefense groups.

10. Barry Kosmin and Seymour Lachman's *One Nation under God* (New York: Harmony Books, 1993), estimates that there are 8,000 followers of Wicca and 20,000 New Agers in America. Many of these are Mystical Deep Ecologists. Including movements like Sun Bear's Bear Tribe, Ananda Marga, the New Communities movement, and nonaffiliated neopaganism, the 20,000-plus estimate seems realistic.

Appendix A: Tables

Table 1
The Four Horsemen of the Green Apocalypse: Violence, Ecological Destruction, Injustice, and Alienation

Spretnak[1]—We live in a society full of:

Violence	Environmental Destruction	Injustice	Alienation
ill will	polluted aquifers	dominance	emptiness
distortion	disregard for limits	hierarchy	indistinguishable blobs
horror	alienation from nature	injustice	mechanistic cogs
rebellion	disastrous results	structural violence	haunting insecurity
manipulation	nuclear holocaust	misogyny	suppression of empathy
Nazis	ecologic crisis	manipulation	spiritual poverty
squelched talk	ecological subjugation	patriarchy	resentment
mechanistic control	dying lakes	gargantuan corporations	anxiety
unyielding rage	species extinction	submission	monoculture
destruction	ecocide	hyper-masculinization	nature alienation
	topsoil loss		no inner life

Foreman[2]—We live in a society full of:

Violence	Environmental Destruction	Injustice	Alienation
tree spiking	upset climates	workers as servants	androids
habitat destruction	poaching	unjust economic systems	frozen passions
ecoterrorism	poisoning the oceans	gilded chains	bumpkin proletariats
life destruction	high extinction rate	imperialism	robotization
perilous times	greenhouse effect	totalitarianism	insane human society
conquest	strip mining	domestication	dullness
sabotage	end of vertebrate evolution	greed	suppression

destruction	overgrazing	manipulation	narrow alternatives
battle for life	ozone depletion	maldistribution	gray bureaucracy
war against the earth	loss of biodiversity	economic captivity	tiredness
FBI harassment	clear-cutting	cooptation	no imagination
terror	erosion	elites	artificial society
crisis	war on large mammals		dulled expectations

Bookchin[3]—We live in a society full of:

Violence	Environmental Destruction	Injustice	Alienation
revolution	excess population	racism	everything lost
domination	clear-cutting	overcrowding	confusion
totalitarianism	pollution	corporate exploitation	antihuman tendencies
war	rain forest destruction	chauvinism	ethics of lesser evils
exotic weapons	ozone depletion	social dislocations	uncertainty
surveillance	water pollution	subjugation	lost faith
imperialism	cancer	sadistic misanthropy	lack of purpose
exploitation	simplified ecosystems	powerful corporate elites	ambiguity
police states	CO_2 buildup	authoritarianism	self-subjugation
fascism	food additives	unfeeling parochialism	disempowerment
bitterly divided societies	acid rain	power politics	no meaning
chaos	grow or die attitude	famine	mindless consumption
oppression	agricultural poisons	social domination	lack of clarity
	ecological ruin	hierarchy	lack of idealism
	plunder of the planet	concentration of ownership	technocratic bureaucracy
	water pollution	reactionaries	lack of social identity
	extinction	cold bureaucratic agencies	pessimism toward civilization

Note: This table lists factors in the critique of modern society as expressed by leading theorists in the three subcultures of the American Green Movement. *Sources:* 1. Derived from Charlene Spretnak's *The Spiritual Dimension of Green Politics* (Santa Fe: Bear and Company, 1986); 2. Derived from David Foreman's *Confessions of an Eco-Warrior* (New York: Harmony Books, 1991); 3. Derived from Murray Bookchin's *Remaking Society* (New York: Black Rose Books, 1989).

Table 2
Selective Summary of Four Planks in the American Green
Movement's National Program

COMMUNITY

The Green Critique of the Present

The old, poor, and marginal are
  categorized as losers
Anthropocentric point of view

The Green Vision

Community as extended family
Interconnection and coexistence
  stressed
Diversity valued and celebrated
Social responsibility for all
Human beings seen as inherently
  good, loving, worthy, and co-
  operative
Geocentric and biocentric values
  stressed
Bioregional awareness emphasized
Support for the arts

Green Strategy

Local face-to-face relationships
Global community of communities
Democratic self-determination
Nonhumans as community members
Stewardship
Ritualization

PEACE AND NONVIOLENCE

The Green Critique of the Present

Poverty is linked to militarism
First world supports most violence
Nation-state derives from patriarchy
  and militarism

LAND USE

The Green Critique of the Present

Materialism and consumerism put
  pressure upon our limited land and
  resources
Population growth (including migra-
  tion) puts pressure upon limited land
  and resources

The Green Vision

We share the land with other life forms
Communities must collectively decide
  how to use the land
Sustainable development must be
  stressed
There is an inherent right of nature to
  exist
Planned land-use policies
Human-scale communities

Green Strategy

Deemphasize automobiles
Think globally, act locally
Regional coordination
Democratic decision making
Reduce/reuse/recycle
Social ownership of land
Stop land speculation

SOCIAL JUSTICE

The Green Critique of the Present

Everything is to be sold
Progress equals destruction
Dominant culture is life denying
Dominant culture separates us through

Corporate, governmental, and
academic elites perpetuate violence
Lack of access to food, land, meaningful work, justice, and education are
forms of violence

racism, sexism, hetrosexism, and class
oppression
The most intense environmental degradation destroys the life and communities of people of color
Men also suffer from the way our
society is structured
Consumerism is directed largely at
women
Women continue to be viewed as different, special, or inferior in important
social, economic and political ways

The Green Vision

Decision making at the lowest
possible level
Civilian-based defense
Mediation

The Green Vision

A multicultural, multiethnic movement
to create a life affirming society
Elimination of sexual harrassment
Equitable empowerment of all citizens
Cultivation of personal, social, and
environmental relations that will help
women welcome the gift of life
Coercion against abortion is not mor-
ally or politically appropriate

Green Strategy

Nonviolent means are always prefer-
able to violent ones
Means and ends are inseparable
Challenge structural violence of all
kinds: individual, family, bioregional,
national, biospheric
Establishment of counterinstitutions
Support conscientious objection
Ecology, not militarism, should inform
public policy

Green Strategy

Greens believe a feminist perspective
is crucial to our survivial
Alternative means of paying for child
care
End advertising that exploits women
Recognition of uneven burden of
poverty on women and children
Creation of a partnership/feminist
culture
Affirmation of the innate humanity,
dignity, and worth of lesbian, gay,
and bisexual people and their full
civil rights
Diversity, cooperation, and gentleness
must be stressed
Opposition to institutional, interpersonal, and cultural racism
Paid maternity/paternity leave of 1 year
or more

Source: Derived from the Greens/Green Party USA's *The Greens/Green Party USA Program*
(Camden NJ: Prompt Press, 1992).

Table 3
The Green Worldview and the Dominant Worldview: Three Levels of Difference

THE PERCEPTUAL LEVEL		THE STRUCTURAL LEVEL	
The Dominant Worldview	The Green Worldview	The Dominant Worldview	The Green Worldview
Aggressive	Cooperative	Packaged knowledge	Understanding
Individualistic	Communitarian	Institutionalized violence	Nonviolence
Reductionist	Integrated and holistic	Production for profit	Production for use
Outer motivated	Inner motivated	High income differentials	Low income gap
Unquestioning use of technology	Discriminating use of technology	Free-market economy	Production for need
Nature is hierarchical	Nature is participatory	Demand stimulation	Voluntary simplicity
Anthropocentric	Biocentric	Capital intensive	Labor intensive
Dominance oriented	Seeks harmony	Centralization	Decentralization
Earth as resource	Earth has intrinsic value	Economies of scale	Human scale
Simplistic uniformity	Diversity	Hierarchical structures	Nonhierarchical
Rigidity	Flexibility	Dependence on experts	Personal participation
Time constraints	Timelessness	Representative democracy	Direct democracy
Mechanistic perception	Systems perception	Nuclear power	Renewable energy
Linear thinking	Nonlinear thinking	High energy consumption	Conservation
Materialistic	Spiritualistic	High technology	Low technology
Objective science	Value-based science	Regulation	Experimentation
Deterministic future	Many possible futures	Isolated products	Interrelated processes
		Unsustainability	Sustainability
		Growth	Self-organization
		Wasteful consumption	Self-regulation
		Concentration of wealth	Redistribution

THE VALUE LEVEL

The Dominant Worldview	The Green Worldview
Materialism	Spirituality
Anthropocentrism	Biocentrism
Patriarchal values	Feminist values
Economic growth	Sustainability/quality
Expansion	Self-regulation
Demand stimulation	Voluntary simplicity
Law and order	Libertarianism
Domination	Harmony
Environmentalism	Ecology
Environment as resource	Intrinsic worth

THE VALUE LEVEL

The Dominant Worldview	The Green Worldview
Consumerism	Enoughness/recycling
Short-term absolutism	Long-term trends
Good/bad dualities	Neutralism
Reliance on external subsidies	Self-reliance
Exploitation	Social justice
Rationality	Intuition
Materialism	Inner growth
Competition	Cooperation
Values experts	Self-reliance
Self-assertion	Social justice

Sources: This chart is derived from several major Green texts, including: Jonathon Porritt, *Seeing Green* (Oxford: Basil Blackwell, 1985), 216-17; Bill Devall and George Sessions, *Deep Ecology* (Salt Lake City: Peregine Smith Books, 1985), 69; Chris Maser, *The Re-designed Forest* (San Pedro, CA: R & E Miles, 1988), 3-59; and Fritjov Capra, *The Turning Point* (New York: Bantam Books, 1983), 389-419.

Table 4.
Countries with Green Parties or Organized Green Movements

Australia	Great Britain	Northern Ireland
Austria	Greece	Norway
Azerbaijan	Holland	Philippines
Belgium	Hong Kong	Poland
Brazil	Ireland	Portugal
Bulgaria	Italy	Romania
Canada	Ivory Coast	Russia
Catalonia	Japan	Scotland
Chile	Latvia	Slovakia
Czech Republic	Lebanon	South Korea
Denmark	Lithuania	Spain
Egypt	Luxembourg	Sweden
Estonia	Malta	Switzerland
Finland	Mexico	Turkey
France	Mongolia	United States
Germany	New Zealand	

Source: Derived from Mike Feinstein, *Sixteen Weeks with the European Greens* (San Pedro, CA: R & E Miles, 1992).

Table 5
The Minority Tradition versus the Dominant Worldview

THE MINORITY TRADITION	THE DOMINANT WORLDVIEW
Decentralized	Centralized
Nonhierarchical	Authority-based
Small scale community	Bureaucratized
Local autonomy	Police
Self-responsibility	Individualism
Democratic	Radical subjectivism
Leadership by example	Leadership by violence
Helping others	Competition
Mutual aid	Deluxe nilhism
Communalism	Consumerism
Self-regulation	Government regulation
Spiritual-religious mentors	Secular authority
Tolerance of a variety of approaches to being	Monopoly of ideology
Open communication with nature	Nature perceived as "data," natural resource
Community fully participates in rituals	Churches monopolize rituals
Broad definition of community, including animals and plants, and an intuition of organic wholeness	Narrow definition of citizenship, all other inhabitants are slaves or disenfranchised
Simplicity of wants	Frequent encouragement to produce more

Source: Derived from Bill Devall and George Sessions,*Deep Ecology* (Salt Lake City: Peregine Smith Books, 1985), 18-19.

Table 6
Eutopian Traits in Green Subcultures

	Neo-Primitivism	Mystical Deep Ecology	Social Ecology
ECOLOGICAL RELATIONS	Biocentric egalitarianism	Biocentric egalitarianism	Benevolent service to further evolution
	Strict limits on manipulation of nature	Nature worship	Ecologically aware manipulation of nature
SOCIAL JUSTICE			
Economics	Nonmaterialist survivalism	Nonmaterialist communitatianism	Materialist egalitarianism
Community	Tribal	Sectarian	Communitarian
Social Roles	Gender neutral	Gender specific	Gender neutral
Work	Skill oriented	Allocated	Shared
GOVERNMENT			
Form of Democracy	Charismatic egalitarianism	Partnership society with feminist bias	Nonhierarchical egalitarianism
Valued Leadership Positions	Provider	Priestess	Facilitator
	Protector	Shawoman	Teacher
NONVIOLENCE	Violence is ritually limited. Self-control is emphasized.	Aggressive tendencies are repressed. Violence is severely punished.	Active deconstruction and elimination of structural and personal violence.

Source: Derived from chapter 4 of this book.

Table 7
Dystopian Elements within Green Subcultures

	Neo-Primitivism	Mystical Deep Ecology	Social Ecology
ECOLOGICAL RELATIONS	Overhunting Overfishing Overforaging	Overgrazing Soil depletion Trapping and hunting of animal pests	Encouragement of overt environmental manipulation
SOCIAL INJUSTICE	The strong exploit the weak Warrior elites and slavery	Religious hierarchy supports gender-based and role-based oppression	Social intolerance of nonconformity Political correctness rules
SYSTEM OF GOVERNMENT	Dictatorial rule by the strong and charismatic	Dictatorial rule by a hierarchy of priestesses with a strong matrifocal bias	Bureaucratic rule by politically correct Machiavellians
VIOLENCE	Warrior society Views violence as natural and inevitable	Religious, cultural and structural oppression	Structural violence against many forms of individuality

Source: Derived from chapter 5 of this book.

Appendix B: Modern Green Literature

My own interest in Green political thought has parallelled the rise of the American Green movement. I trace my introduction to this field to a graduate-level political science course at the University of Hawaii, Political Design for the Future.[1] The course requirements included an analysis of several different futurists, one of whom was Mark Satin, author of the book *New Age Politics* (1978). *New Age Politics* fascinated me. It spoke of a politics that originated with the heart rather than the traditional power politics stressing manipulation and force of will that I had grown accustomed to during my tenure working with the Washington State and Hawaii State legislatures.

My interest in this new field of politics led to other graduate-level political science courses at the University of Hawaii. Ira Rohter's New Age Politics course introduced me to the vast arena of literature that was the precursor of modern Green political thought in the United States. Among the texts used by Rohter were *The Turning Point* (1982) and *The Tao of Physics* (1984) by Capra, *Politics of the Solar Age* (1981) by Henderson, and *Ecotopia* (1975) by Callenbach. These texts complemented Satin's work by stressing the values of interconnectedness, interdependence, and ecological balance. They also argued that a positive alternative to the materialistic, self-oriented individualism expressed by the dominant culture of the 1980s was possible.

Many other books of this era (1970s and early 1980s) offered the same message in slightly different forms and reached large numbers of people. Reich, *The Greening of America* (1970); Ferguson, *Aquarian Conspiracy* (1980); Schumacher, *Small is Beautiful* (1973); and Bookchin, *Post-Scarcity Anarchism* (1986b); made the best-seller lists. This proto-Green thought (variously described as transformational politics, new political science, new age politics, political ecology, or ecophilosophy) became "the in thing" with major publishing companies, such as Bantam Books, whose New Age Books series included dozens of offerings stressing proto-Green themes.

Then Capra and Spretnak's *Green Politics* (1984) was published. *Green Politics* told the story of Die Grunen, the West German Greens, who not only managed to articulate the frustrations and hopes of many of their time, but also managed to turn these feelings into a political party with the capacity to challenge traditional electoral politics. Capra and Spretnak's book struck a chord in America. *Green Politics* was the first full-length book in the United States to link the four Green values of ecological harmony, social justice, nonviolence, and democratic participation with active politics. This is the point where the field of Green literature as a separate and unique entity in America can be said to have begun. The same year in which *Green Politics* was published, the first nationwide Green network in America was established. A number of periodicals strictly devoted to Green politics and Green political thought in America quickly blossomed in the ensuing years, including *Green Letter*, *Green Synthesis*, and *Green Action*. Dozens of alternative periodicals devoted significant amounts of coverage to the Greens and Green-oriented issues.[2] Academic journals such as *New Politics, Tikkun, Telos,* and *Environmental Ethics* increased their interest in Green-oriented articles, as did the mainstream press.

In the mid-1980s, subcultures within the American Green movement began to distinguish themselves with the help of texts like Tobias, *Deep Ecology* (1985); Devall and Session, *Deep Ecology* (1985); Foreman and Haywood *Ecodefense* (1987); and Bookchin, *The Modern Crisis* (1986a). Subcultures also issued their own newsletters and journals. Session's *Ecophilosophy*, Fox's *Creation*, Foreman's *Earth First! Journal* and the Bookchin-influenced *Green Perspectives* are examples of prominent periodicals aimed at particular Green audiences.[3]

In 1987, Brian Tokar's *The Green Alternative* offered the first book-length analysis of the American Green Movement. *The Green Alternative* was followed by publishing companies such as South End Press and Sierra Club offering titles focusing on the American Greens, examples include Biehl, *Rethinking Ecofeminist Politics*, (1991); Diamond and Orenstein, *Reweaving the World* (1990); and Chase, *Defending the Earth* (1991). New Society Publishers, built entirely around publishing Green books, now publishes close to one hundred Green-oriented titles.

With this boom in Green publishing (and the corresponding boom in activism explored in chapter 3), several major figures have become prominent. Dave Foreman, Chris Manes, Rik Scarce, and Edward Abbey have become synonymous with the Earth First!, eco-warrior stance of Neo-Primitivism. Peter Berg, Paul Shepard, and Gary Snyder represent a more sensitive, but no less confrontational, Neo-Primitivistic relationship to bioregional advocacy. Charlene Spretnak, Starhawk, Paula Gunn Allen, and Deena Metzger have emerged as major Mystical Deep Ecologists. Murray Bookchin, Janet Biehl,

Ynestra King, and Howard Hawkins have risen to the forefront of Social Ecologist thought and activity. All of these people have written major works in the field and all participate in activism as well.[4]

A few authors have tried to transcend subculture affiliation to offer overviews of the American Green movement.[5] Tokar has published several articles since *The Green Alternative* that expand his view of the Greens and explore recent changes in the movement, such as the Social Ecologist attempt to dominate the Green Party/Green Movement USA and increasing factionalism within the Earth First! network. John Resenbrink (1992) has joined the ranks of Tokar with a book-length analysis of the movement entitled *The Greens and the Politics of Transformation*. One significant work in the field that ignores subculture limitations is Ira Rohter, *A Green Hawai'i* (1992). Rohter recognizes that he is attracted to different aspects of each subculture and thus concentrates upon political change from a variety of perspectives without denigrating the worth of alternative methods that the subcultures adopt for social change.

The study of Green politics and cosmology in the United States is a young and exciting field full of opportunities. It is my hope that this book illuminates and encourages innovative ways of thinking about this important new phenomenon. I also hope that it empowers those who read it as much as the books discussed here did for me.[6]

NOTES

1. Taught by Jim Dator, who was then the secretary-general of the World Futures Studies Federation.

2. *Coevolution Quarterly, Utne Reader, New Options*, and *In These Times* are just a few of these. See Donald Davis, *Ecophilosophy* (San Pedro, CA: R & E Miles, 1989), and virtually any issue of *Utne Reader* for a good overview of Green-oriented periodicals.

3. Fox, like many Deep Ecologists, is based in Canada but has a large following in the United States.

4. This brief overview of prominent writers in the various subcultures of the American Green movement is necessarily limited. An annotated listing of subculture authors who deserve recognition here could fill pages. Throughout the book I have tried to include this widespread wealth of diversity rather than concentrating on any one person. The bibliography included should serve as sufficient testimony in this regard. Yet, as you can see, certain individuals, such as David Foreman, Murray Bookchin, and Charlene Spretnak, have made such contributions to their specific subcultures and are so illustrative of subculture ideology that they deservedly receive greater recognition than other subculture contributors. Two people who deserve further mention at this point are William Irwin Thompson, whose course on Green cosmology at the University of Hawaii was an excellent starting point for thinking in a deeper way about the Greens, and Johan Galtung, whose help in the early stages of my work was very heartening.

5. Alston Chase, "The Great, Green, Deep Ecology Revolution," *Rolling Stone*, April 23, 1987, is the only other observer of the American Greens who has discussed

the three subcultures I explore in this book as separate subcultures per se. Bookchin's *Remaking Society* (New York: Black Rose Books, 1989), has critiqued the subcultures of Neo-Primitivism and Mystical Deep Ecology but has not gone further into analysis of how these subcultures fit into the Green movement. Most observers and advocates are like Bookchin, critiquing their competition but not analyzing the roles they fulfill.

6. One of my generational cohorts has remarked that as a baby boomer, he knew if he was going through a certain period or feeling a certain feeling that there were millions of people who were doing the same thing. At the start of my exploration of Green politics, I had been active in traditional electoral politics. I had worked for the senate majority leader of the Washington State Senate, who was a Republican, and the president of the Hawaii State Senate, who was a Democrat. I had achieved moderate success in the business world. Yet the material and status-oriented rewards of the modern age were not enough—somehow something was lacking. Doubts about the current value system of our culture and structure of our society led me to seek possible alternatives. My dissatisfaction coupled with my interest in politics eventually led me to the field of alternative futures and the study of the Greens.

Bibliography

Abbott, Sally. 1990. "The Origins of God in the Blood of the Lamb." In *Reweaving the World*, ed. Irene Diamond and Gloria Feman Orenstein. San Francisco: Sierra Club Books.

Abram, David. 1987. "The Perceptual Implications of Gaia." *ReVision*, Winter/Spring.

Adler, Margot. 1989. "The Juice and the Mystery." In *Healing the Wounds*, ed. Judith Plant. Philadelphia: New Society.

Aiken, William. 1984. "Ethical Issues in Agriculture." In *Earthbound*, ed. Tom Regan. New York: Random House.

Allen, Paula Gunn. 1990. "The Woman I Love is a Planet, The Planet I Love is a Tree." In *Reweaving the World*, ed. Irene Diamond and Gloria Feman Orenstein. San Francisco: Sierra Club Books.

Allin, Craig. 1982. *The Politics of Wilderness Preservation*. Westport CT: Greenwood Press.

Amara, Roy. 1981. "The Futures Field: Searching For Definitions and Boundaries." *The Futurist*, February.

Anderson, Walter Truett. 1987. *To Govern Evolution: Further Adventures of the Political Animal*. Boston: Harcourt Brace Johanovitch.

Andruss, Van, Christopher Plant, Judith Plant, and Eleanor Wright, eds. 1990. *Home! A Bioregional Reader*. Philadelphia: New Society.

Bahro, Rudolf. 1986. *Building the Green Movement*. Philadelphia: New Society.

Bandow, Doug. 1990. "Eco-Terrorism." *The Heritage Foundation Backgrounder*, 764 (April).

Baranoff, Zvi. 1988. "Glastnost for the American Greens." *Green Action* 5, no.3.

Barber, Benjamin. 1984. *Strong Democracy: Participatory Politics for a New Age*. Berkeley: University of California Press.

Bearup-Neal, Sarah. 1990. "Trees: A Misanthropic View." *Earth First! Journal*, November 1.

Beauvoir, Simone. 1974. *The Second Sex*. New York: Vintage Books.

Bell, Daniel. 1973. *The Coming of Post-Industrial Society: A New Venture in Social Forecasting*. New York: Basic Books.

Bell, Wendell. 1985. "Futuristics: A New Field of Inquiry." *Social and Economic Studies* 32, no. 2.
————. Forthcoming. *The Foundations of the Futures Field*.
Berg, Peter. 1990a. "Bioregional and Wild! A New Cultural Image . . ." In *Turtle Talk*, ed. Christopher Plant and Judith Plant. Philadelphia: New Society.
————. 1990b. "More than Just Saving What's Left." In *Home! A Bioregional Reader*, ed. Van Andruss et al. Philadelphia: New Society.
Berg, Peter, Beryl Magilavy, and Seth Zuckerman, eds. 1989. *A Green City Program For San Francisco Bay Area Cities and Towns*. San Francisco: Planet Drum Books.
Berman, Morris. 1981. *The Reenchantment of the World*. Ithaca and London: Cornell University Press.
Berry, Thomas. 1988. *The Dream of the Earth*. San Francisco: Sierra Club Books.
Bertaux, Pierre. 1968. "The Future of Man." In *Environment and Change: The Next Fifty Years*, ed. W. R. Ewald. Bloomington: Indiana University Press.
Betz, Charles. 1992. "Working Groups Reports." *Green Politics* 2, no. 2 (Summer).
Beverly, Robert. [1705] 1947. *The History and Present State of Virginia*. Reprint, Louis B. Wright. Chapel Hill: University of North Carolina Press.
Bezold, Clement, James Dator, Robert Olson, and Jonathon Peck. 1983. *Alternative Futures for U.S. Society*. Alexandria, VA: Institute for Alternative Futures.
Biehl, Janet. 1988. "The Politics of Myth." *Green Perspectives*. Newsletter of the Green Program Project, no. 7 (June).
————. 1991. *Rethinking Ecofeminist Politics*. Boston: South End Press.
Bookchin, Murray. 1980. *Toward An Ecological Society*. Montreal: Black Rose Press.
————. 1981. "The Concept of Social Ecology." *The CoEvolution Quarterly*, Winter.
————. 1982a. *The Ecology of Freedom*. Palo Alto, CA: Chesire Books.
————. 1982b. "Finding the Subject: Notes on Whitebook and 'Habermas Ltd.'" *Telos*, no. 52 (Summer).
————. 1985a. "Radicalizing Democracy." Interview, *Kick It Over*. Burlington, VT: Green Program Project.
————. 1985b. "Radical Social Ecology." *Harbinger*, no. 3.
————. 1985c. "What is Social Ecology?" *Alternatives* 12, no. 3/4 (Spring/Summer).
————. 1986a. *The Modern Crisis*. Philadelphia: New Society.
————. 1986b. *Post-Scarcity Anarchism*. Montreal: Black Rose Press.
————. 1987a. "Crisis in the Ecology Movement." Distributed at the Green Gathering, Eugene, Oregon.
————. 1987b. "Social Ecology Versus 'Deep-Ecology': A Challenge for the Ecology Movement." *Green Perspectives*, no. 4 and 5 (Summer).
————. 1987c. "Thinking Ecologically: A Dialectical Approach." *Our Generation* 18, no. 2, (Spring/Summer).
————. 1988a. *Ecology and Revolutionary Thought*. Burlington VT: Green Program Project.
————. 1988b. "A Reply to my Critics." *Green Synthesis*, December.
————. 1988c. "Toward a Philosophy of Nature." In *Deep Ecology* ed. Michael Tobias, San Marcos, CA: Avant Books.
————. 1989. *Remaking Society*. New York: Black Rose Books.
————. 1990. "Cities, Councils and Confederations." In *Turtle Talk*, ed. Christopher Plant and Judith Plant. Philadephia: New Society.

Booth, Kelly. 1990. "How Humans Adapt." In *Home! A Bioregional Reader*, ed. Van Andruss et al. Philadelphia: New Society.

Boyte, H. C. 1980. *The Backyard Revolution*. Philadelphia: Temple University Press.

Bradford, George. 1989. *How Deep is Deep Ecology?* Hadley, MA: Times Change Press.

Bramwell, Anna. 1989. *Ecology in the Twentieth Century: A History*. New Haven and London: Yale University Press.

Broom, Leonard. 1981. *Sociology*. New York: Harper & Row.

Brown, Lester, ed. 1985-1993. *The State of the World Atlas*. New York: Norton.

Callenbach, Ernest. 1975. *Ecotopia*. New York: Bantam Books.

———. 1989. *Ecotopia Emerging*. New York: Bantam Books.

Cameron, Anne. 1989. "First Mother and the Rainbow Children." In *Healing the Wounds*, ed. Judith Plant. Philadelphia: New Society.

Campbell, Ena. 1982. "The Virgin of Guadelupe and the Female Self-Image." In *Mother Worship*, ed. J. P. Preston, Chapel Hill: University of North Carolina Press.

Campbell, Joseph, with Bill Moyers. 1988. *The Power of the Myth*. New York: Doubleday.

Canan, Penelope, and George Pring. 1988. "Strategic Lawsuits against Public Participation." *Social Problems*, no. 35 (December).

Capra. Fritjof. 1982. *The Turning Point: Science, Society and the Rising Culture*. New York: Bantam Books.

———. 1984. *The Tao of Physics*. New York: Bantam Books.

———. 1986a. "The Concept of Paradigm and Paradigm Shift." *ReVision*, Summer/Fall.

———. 1986b. "The Turning Point: Crisis and Transformation in Science and Society." Paper presented at the University of Hawaii Political Science Colloquium, Honolulu.

Capra, Fritjof, and Charlene Spretnak. 1984. *Green Politics*. New York: Dutton.

Carragee, Kevin M. 1991. "News and Ideology." *Journalism Monographs*, no. 128 (August).

Carson, Rachel. 1962. *Silent Spring*. New York: Fawcett Crest.

Chandler, William, and Alan Siaroff. 1986. "Post-Industrial Politics in Germany and the Origins of the Greens." *Comparative Politics* (April).

Chase, Alston. 1987. "The Great, Green, Deep-Ecology Revolution." *Rolling Stone*, April 23.

Chase, Steve, ed. 1991. *Defending the Earth: A Dialogue between Murray Bookchin and Dave Foreman*. Boston: South End Press.

Chau, Simon. 1988. "Why Green Power?" Interview distributed by Hong Kong Green Power, February.

Cheney, Jim. 1987. "Ecofeminism and Deep Ecology." *Environmental Ethics* 9, no. 2 (Summer).

Chollette, Kathryn, Ross Dobson, Kent Gerecke, Marcia Nozick, Roberta Simpson, and Linda Williams. 1989. "Green City: An Introduction." *City Magazine 2*, no. 1 (Summer/Winter).

Christ, Carol. 1990. "Rethinking Theology and Nature." In *Reweaving the World: The Emergence of Ecofeminism*, ed. Irene Diamond and Gloria Feman Orenstein. San Francisco: Sierra Club Books.

Christian, James. 1981. *Philosophy*. New York: Holt, Rinehart & Winston.

Churchill, Ward. 1988. *Agents of Repression*. Boston: South End Press.

C. M. 1990. "An Appraisal of Monkeywrenching." *Earth First! Journal*, February 2.

Conner, Daniel Keith. 1988. "Is AIDS the Answer to an Environmentalist's Prayer?" *Utne Reader*, May-June.

Cooney, Robert, and Helen Michalowski. 1987. *Power to the People*. Philadelphia: New Society.

Cronon, William. 1983. *Changes in the Land*. New York: Hill & Wang.

D'Anieri, Paul, Claire Ernst, and Elizabeth Kier. 1990. "New Social Movements in Historical Perspective." *Comparative Politics* 22, no. 4 (July).

Dator, James. 1974a. "Futuristics and the Exercise of Anticipatory Democracy in Hawaii." In *Political Science and the Study of the Future*, ed. A. Somit. Hinsdale, IL: Dryden Press.

————. 1974b. "Neither There nor Then: A Eutopian Alternative to the Development Model of Future Society." In *Human Futures*, ed. Eleanora Masini. London: IPC Science and Technology Press.

————. 1975. "Decolonizing the Future." In *The Next 25 Years*, ed. Andrew Spekke. New York: World Future Society.

————. 1978. "Futures Research." In *Malaysia 200 : A Preliminary Inquiry*, ed. Bruce Ross-Larson. Kuala Lampur: Syed Kechik Foundation.

————. 1979. "The Futures of Cultures/Cultures of the Future." In *Perspectives in Cross-Cultural Psychology*, ed. Anthony Marsella. New York: Academic Press.

————. 1983. "Loose Connections: A Vision of a Transformational Society." In *Visions of Desirable Societies*, ed. Eleanora Masini. Oxford: Pergamon Press.

————. 1987. "Futures of Development and Development of the Future." Paper presented at "Development of the Asia-Pacific Region," conference sponsored by the Friedrich-Nauman-Stifting Foundation, November 20.

————. 1991. "Participating with the Universe." Paper presented at the World Futures Studies Federation XII World Conference in Barcelona, Spain, September.

————. 1993. "Dogs Don't Bark at Parked Cars." Presented at the World Futures Studies Federation XIII World Conference in Turku, Finland, August 23.

Davis, Donald Edward. 1989. *Ecophilosophy: A Field Guide to the Literature*. San Pedro, CA: R & E Miles.

Degler, Carl. 1977. *The Age of the Ecoomic Revolution 1876-1900*. Glenview, IL: Scott, Foresman.

Detroit Summer Coalition, The. 1992. "Detroit Summer," *Green Politics*, Summer.

Devall, Bill. n.d. "Interview with Dave Foreman." *Simply Living* 2, no. 12.

Devall, Bill and George Sessions. 1985. *Deep Ecology*. Salt Lake City: Peregrine Smith Books.

Diamond, Irene and Gloria Feman Orenstein, eds. 1990. *Reweaving the World: The Emergence of Ecofeminism*. San Francisco: Sierra Club Books.

Dittmers, Manuel. 1986. *The Green Party in West Germany*. Oxford, UK: University Printing House.

Dobson, Andrew. 1990. *Green Political Thought*. Boston: Unwin Hyman.

Dodge, Jim. 1990. "Living By Life: Some Bioregional Theory and Practice." In *Home!: A Bioregional Reader*, ed. Van Andruss et al. Philadelphia: New Society.

Douglas, Jack. 1973. *Introduction to Sociology*. New York: Free Press.

Dryzek, John S. 1990. "Green Reason: Communicative Ethics for the Biosphere." *Environmental Ethics* 12, no. 3 (Fall).

D'Souza, Corinne Kumar. 1989. "A New Movement, A New Hope." In *Healing the Wounds*, ed. Judith Plant. Philadelphia: New Society.

Dubos, Rene. 1980. *The Wooing of the Earth*. New York: Scribner's.

Dudley, Michael Kioni. 1990. *Man, Gods, and Nature*. Honolulu: Na Kane O Ka Malo Press.

Dwight, Timothy. [1821] 1989. *Travels in New England and New York*. Reprint, ed. Barbara Miller Solomon. Cambridge: MIT Press.

Eaton, Randall, ed. 1985. *The Human/Animal Connection*. Incline Village, NV: Carnivore Journal and Sierra College Press.

————. 1987. "Hunting and the Great Mystery of Nature." *Utne Reader*, January-February.

Eckersley, Robin. 1989. "Divining Evolution: The Ecological Ethics of Murray Bookchin." *Environmental Ethics* 11, no. 2 (Summer).

Eggleston, Edward. 1888. *History of the United States and Its Peoples*. New York: American Book Company.

Ehrenberg, Margaret. 1989. *Women in Prehistory*. Norman, OK: University of Oklahoma Press.

Eisler, Riane. 1987. *The Chalice and the Blade*. New York: Harper & Row.

————. 1990. "The Gaia Tradition and the Partnership Future: An Ecofeminist Manifesto." In *Reweaving the World*, ed. Irene Diamond and Gloria Feman Orenstein. San Francisco: Sierra Club Books.

Elder, Klaus. 1982. "A New Social Movement?" *Telos,* no. 52 (Summer).

Ely, John. 1986. "The Greens of West Germany: An Alternative Modernity (Or: How German is it?)." Paper presented at the Annual Convention of the American Political Science Association, Washington, DC, August 28.

Estes, Caroline. 1990. "Consensus and Community." In *Turtle Talk*, ed. Christopher Plant and Judith Plant. Philadelphia: New Society.

"Europe's Choice." 1983. *The Economist,* February 26.

Feinstein, Mike. 1992. *Sixteen Weeks with the European Greens*. San Pedro, CA: R & E Miles.

Ferguson, Marilyn. 1980. *The Aquarian Conspiracy*. J. P. Tarcher/St. Martin's Press.

Ferkiss, Victor. 1993. *Nature, Technology, and Society: Cultural Roots of the Current Environmental Crisis*. London: Adamine Press.

Fleming, Pat, and Joanna Macy. 1990. "The Council of All Beings." In *Home! A Bioregional Reader*, ed. Van Andruss et al. Philadelphia: New Society.

Fletcher, Geoffrey. 1979. "Key Concepts in the Futures Perspective." *World Future Society Bulletin*, January-February.

Flexner, Eleanor. 1974. *Century of Struggle*. New York: Atheneum.

Flynn, Andrew, and Phillip Lowe. 1992. "The Future of Green Parties in Britain, France and Germany." In *Green Politics Two*, ed. Wolfgang Rudig. Edinburgh: Edinburgh University Press.

Foreman, David. 1990. "Now's the Time." *Mother Jones*, April-May.

————. 1991. *Confessions of An Eco-Warrior*. New York: Harmony Books.

Foreman, David and Dave Haywood, eds. 1987. *Ecodefense: A Field Guide to Monkeywrenching*. Tucson, AZ: Earth First! Books.

Galtung, Johan. 1986. "The Green Movement: A Socio-Historical Exploration." *International Sociology* 1, no. 1 (March).

Gilbert, Matthew. 1988. "Keep the Spirit Alive." *Green Synthesis*, no. 29 (December).

Gimbutas, Marjita. 1982a. *The Godesses and Gods of Old Europe, 6500-3500 B.C.: Myths and Cult Images*. London: Thames and Hudson.

———. 1982b. "Women and Culture in Goddess-Oriented Old Europe." In *The Politics of Women's Spirituality*, ed. Charlene Spretnak. New York: Anchor Books.

Glasser, William. 1975. *The Identity Society*. New York: Harper & Row.

Goodwyn, Lawrence. 1976. *Democratic Promise: The Populist Movement in America*. New York: Oxford University Press.

Gore, Al. 1992. *Earth in the Balance*. Boston: Houghton Mifflin.

Gramsci, A. 1971. *Prison Notebooks*. New York: International Publishers.

"The Green Guerrilla." 1991. *Entertainment Weekly*, March 22.

"The Green Movement/Bioregional Connection." 1988. *Green Letter* 4, no. 4 (Fall).

Green Party Political Association of British Columbia. 1988. *Condensed Policy*. Vacouver, BC. June.

"Green Voting Resources." 1992. *Utne Reader*, no. 53 (September-October).

Greens Clearinghouse Staff. 1992. "The Greens in '91-92." *Green Politics* 2, no. 2 (Summer).

"Greens Win 560,000 votes in 1992, Seat 11 Candidates." N.d. Press Release. *The Greens/Green Party USA*.

The Greens/Green Party USA. 1992. "*The Green Program*." Camden, NJ: Prompt Press.

Griffin, Donald. 1984. *Animal Thinking*. Cambridge, MA: Harvard University Press.

Griffin, Susan. 1978. *Women and Nature: The Roaring Inside Her*. New York: Harper & Row.

———. 1989. "Split Culture." In *Healing the Wounds*, ed. Judith Plant. Philadelphia: New Society.

———. 1990. "Curves along the Road." In *Reweaving the World*, ed. Irene Diamond and Gloria Feman Orenstein. San Francisco: Sierra Club Books.

Gwaganad. 1989. "Speaking for the Earth." In *Healing the Wounds*, ed. Judith Plant. Philadelphia: New Society.

Habermas, Jurgen. 1971. *Knowledge and Human Interests*. Boston: Beacon Press.

———. 1975. *Legitimation Crisis*. Boston: Beacon Press.

———. 1979a. *Communication and the Evolution of Society*. Boston: Beacon Press.

———. 1979b. "Consciousness-Raising or Redemptive Criticism?" *New German Critique* 17.

———. 1979c. "The Crisis of Late Capitalism and the Future of Democracy." *Telos*, no. 39.

———. 1981a. "The Dialectics of Rationality: Interview with Axel Honeth, Eberhard Knodler-Bunte, and Arno Widmann." *Telos*, no. 49.

———. 1981b. "New Social Movements." *Telos*, no. 49.

———. 1982. "Reply to My Critics." In *Habermas: Critical Debates*, ed. John B. Thompson and David Held. Cambridge, MA: MIT Press.

———. 1984, 1987. *The Theory of Communicative Action* 1 and 2. Boston: Beacon Press.

———. 1988. "Questions and Counterquestions." In *Habermas and Modernity*, ed. Richard Bernstein. Cambridge, MA: MIT Press.

Harman, Willis. 1990. *Global Mind Change*. New York: Warner Books.

Havel, Vaclav. 1985. *The Power of the Powerless*. Ed. John Keane. Armock, New York: Sharpe, 1985.

————. 1988. *"Anti-Political Politics."* In Civil Society and the State, ed. John Keane. London/New York: Verso.

Hawken, Paul. 1982. *Seven Tomorrows: Toward Voluntary History.* New York: Bantam Books.

Hawkins, Howard. 1988. "The Potential of the Green Movement." *New Politics* 2, no. 1 (New Series, Summer).

Hay, P. R. 1992. "Vandals at the Gate: The Tasmanian Greens and the Perils of Power Sharing." In *Green Politics Two,* ed. Wolfgang Rudig. Edinbugh: Edinburgh University Press.

Henderson, Hazel. 1981. *Politics of the Solar Age.* Garden City, NY: Anchor Press/Doubleday.

Hendricks, Evan. 1988. *Former Secrets.* No Address Available: Campaign For Political Rights.

Henningsen, Manfred. 1992. "Democracy or the Promise of 'Civil Society.'" In *Linking Present Decisions to Long-range Visions,* ed. Mika Mannermaa. Turku, Finland: World Futures Studies Federation.

Herbert, Nick. 1985. *Quantum Reality.* New York: Doubleday.

Hertzler, Joyce. 1928. *Social Progress.* New York: The Century Company.

Hildebrandt, Kai, and Russell Dalton. 1978. "The New Politics." In *Elections and Parties,* ed. Mx Kaase. London and Beverly Hills: Sage.

Hill, Phil. 1985. "Crisis of the Greens." *Radical America* 19, no. 5.

Hill, Phil, and Howard Hawkins. 1988. "Dana Beal's 'Mid-Atlantic Greens' Are Bad News, but Not Because They Smoke Too Much Dope." *Green Synthesis,* no. 28 (September).

Hobbes, Thomas. [1651] 1972. *Leviathan.* In *Communism, Fascism and Democracy,* ed. Carl Cohen. New York: Random House.

Huber, Bettina. 1978. "Images of the Future." In *The Procedures of Futures Research,* ed. Jib Fowles. Westport, CT: Greenwood Press.

Hueber, Graham. 1991. "Americans Report High Levels of Environmental Concern, Activity." *The Gallup Poll Monthly,* no. 307 (April).

Hughes, J. 1989. "Greens and Socialists: It Takes Two to Tango." *The Activist,* no. 24 (March-April).

Hunter, Bob. 1988. "Ecology as Religion." *Ecolution* 2, no. 4 (October).

Huntington, Samuel. 1968. *Political Order in a Changing Society.* New Haven, CT: Yale University Press.

Inglehart, Ronald. 1977. *The Silent Revolution.* Princeton, NJ: Princeton University Press.

————. 1985. "New Perspectives on Value Change." *Comparative Political Studies,* no. 17.

Institute for Social Ecology. 1987-1994. *Summer Semester Prospectives.* Rochester, VT: Institute for Social Ecology.

"International Greens." 1993. *Hawai'i Green Party News.* September.

Isaak, Alan. 1987. *An Introduction to Politics.* Glenview, IL: Scott, Foresman.

Jacobs, Lynn. 1989. "Letters to the Editor." *Earth First! Journal,* November 1.

James, E. O. 1959. *The Cult of the Mother Goddess: An Archeological and Documentary Study.* London: Thames & Hudson.

Jancar, Barbara. 1992. "Chaos as an Explanation of the Role of Environmental Groups in East European Politics." In *Green Politics Two*, ed. Wolfgang Rudig. Edinburgh: Edinburgh Press.

Johnson, Gail. N. d. "Patriarchal Domination of Women, Nature and Animals." *Feminists for Animal Liberation Newsletter* 4, nos. 1-2 (Spring-Summer).

Jones, Christopher. 1989. "Gaia Futures: The Emerging Mythology and Politics of the Earth." Ph.D. dissertation, Department of Political Science, University of Hawaii.

————. 1992. "The Manoa School of Futures Studies." *Futures Research Quarterly* 8, no. 4 (Winter).

Josephson, Matthew. 1962. *The Robber Barons*. New York: Harcourt, Brace & World.

Kahn, Herman, and John B. Phelps. 1967. *The Year 2000; A Framework for Speculation on the Next Thirty-three Years*. New York: Macmillan.

Kassman, Kenn. 1986. "Green Paper Number One." Paper prepared for Political Science 699, University of Hawaii, Fall.

————. 1987. "Building the Hawaii Green Movement." Paper prepared for Political Science 699, University of Hawaii, Spring.

————. 1989a. "Beyond Enlightenment: The Greening of Hawaii?" Paper presented at the School of Hawaiian, Asian and Pacific Studies Conference *Emerging Themes in Hawaii, Asia and the Pacific*, April.

————. 1989b. "The Future of the American Green Movement as a Political/Social Change Agent!" Paper presented at the University of Hawaii Political Science Department Colloqium Series on International Politics, Summer.

————. 1989c. "Post-Enlightenment Politics—The American Green Movement and the Search for a New Rationality," *Occasional Papers in Political Science* 3, no. 1 (August).

————. 1990a. "Aina, Ohana, Aloha, and Politics: The Relevance of Traditional Hawaiian Values for a Post-Modern World." *Futura*, April.

————. 1990b. "American Cultural Perceptions and the Future of Nature." Paper presented at the University of Hawaii Political Science Department Colloquium Series: *Politics and the Natural Environment*, January.

————. 1990c. "The American Green Movement—Vision in Search of Praxis." Paper presented at the World Future Studies Federation XIth World Conference, Budapest, Hungary, May.

————. 1993. "Envisioning a New America: The Theory, Praxis and Future Visions of Three Subcultures in the American Green Movement." Paper presented at the WFSF XIII Conference in Turku, Finland, August.

————. 1994. "Who Killed Mother Nature?" Review of *Nature, Technology and Society: Cultural Roots of the Current Environmental Crisis*, by Victor Ferkiss. *Futures* 26, no. 3, April.

————. 1995a. "What is to be Done?: A Different Way of Viewing the Future." Review of *To Nonviolent Political Science, by* Glenn Paige and *Crucial Questions About the Future*, by Alan Tough. *New Renaissance* 5, no. 3.

————. 1995b. "Who is Responsible for the Current Environmental Crisis?" Review of *Nature, Technology and Society,* by Victor Ferkiss. *New Renaissance* 5, no. 2.

————. 1996a. "Protecting and Greening the Future." Review of *A Green Hawai'i*, by Ira Rohter and *The New Protectionism*, by Lang and Hines. *New Renaissance* 6, no. 1.

———. 1996b. "Searching For Alternative Futures." Review of *The Foresight Principle, by* Richard Slaughter. *New Renaissance* 6, no. 2.

Keller, Mara Lyn. 1990. "The Eleusinian Mysteries." In *Reweaving the World*, ed. Irene Diamond and Gloria Feman Orenstein. San Francisco: Sierra Club Books.

Kelly, Petra. 1984. *Fighting for Hope*. Boston: South End Press.

———. 1991. "The Future of the German Greens." *Green Letter/Greener Times*, no. 27 (Spring).

———. 1992. *Nonviolence Speaks to Power*. Ed. Glenn Paige and Sarah Gilliat. Honolulu: Center for Global Nonviolence Planning Project, Spark M. Matsunaga Institute for Peace.

Kessler, Carol Farley. 1990. "Bibliography of Utopian Fiction by United States Women 1836-1988." *Utopian Studies* 1, no. 1.

Kheel, Marti. 1985. "The Liberation of Nature:A Circular Affair." *Environmental Ethics* 7, no. 2 (Summer).

———. 1989. "From Healing Herbs to Deadly Drugs: Western Medicine's War against the Natural World." In *Healing the Wounds*, ed. Judith Plant. Philadelphia: New Society, 1989.

———. 1990. "Ecofeminism and Deep Ecology." In *Reweaving the World*, ed. Irene Diamond and Gloria Feman Orenstein. San Francisco: Sierra Club Books.

King, Ynestra. 1988. "Coming of Age with the Greens." *Z Magazine* 1, no. 2 (February).

———. 1990a. "The Ecology of Feminism and the Feminism of Ecology." In *What Is Ecofeminism?* ed. Gwyn Kirk. New York: Ecofeminist Resources.

———. 1990b. "Healing the Wounds." In *Reweaving the World*, ed. Irene Diamond and Gloria Feman Orenstein. San Francisco: Sierra Club Books.

"Kohl Calls for Party Unity and Fighting Spirit at CDU National Convention." 1994. *This Week in Germany*. February 25.

Kosmin, Barry, and Seymour Lachman. 1993. *One Nation under God*. New York: Harmony Books.

Kropotkin, Peter. N.d. *Mutual Aid*. Boston: Porter Sargent.

Kuhn, Thomas. 1962. *The Structure of Scientific Revolutions*. Chicago: University of Chicago Press.

LaChapelle, Dolores. 1988. "Sacred Land, Sacred Sex." In *Deep Ecology*, ed. Michael Tobias. San Marcos, CA: Avant Books.

———. 1989. "Sacred Land, Sacred Sex." In *Healing the Wounds*, ed. Judith Plant. Philadelphia: New Society.

Leacock, Eleanor. 1987. "Women in Egalitarian Societies." In *Becoming Visible*, ed. Renate Bridenthal, et al. Boston: Houghton Mifflin.

LeGuin, Ursula. 1989. "Women/Wilderness." In *Healing the Wounds*, ed. Judith Plant, Philadelphia: New Society.

Leiss, William. 1989. "The Myth of the Information Society." In *Cultural Politics in Contemporary America*, ed. Ian Angus and Sut Jhally. New York: Routledge.

Leopold, Aldo. 1949. *Sand County Almanac*. Oxford: Oxford University Press.

Link, Aurthur. 1954. *Woodrow Wilson and The Progressive Era*. New York: Harper & Row.

Linton, Michael and Thomas Greco. 1990. "LETS: The Local Exchange Trading System." In *Home!*, ed. Van Andruss, et al. Philadelphia: New Society.

Liptak, Karen. 1991. *Indians of the Pacific Northwest*. New York: Facts on File.

Live Wild or Die! 1988. "Smoke Weed." San Francisco, California: Live Wild or Die! February.

Livingston, John. 1981. *The Fallacy of Wildlife Conservation.* New Marlcet, Ontario: McCelland and Steward Ltd.

"Local Green Updates." 1992. *Green Politics* 2, no. 2 (Summer).

Locke, John. [1640] 1972. *Second Treatise of Government.* In *Communism, Fascism and Democracy,* ed. Carl Cohen. New York: Random House.

Los Angeles News Service. 1989. "FBI Probed Critics of Library Checks." *Honolulu Star Bulletin and Advertiser,* November 5.

Lovelock, James. 1979. *Gaia: A New Look at Life on Earth.* Oxford: Oxford University Press.

————. 1988. *The Ages of Gaia: A Biography of Our Living Earth.* New York: Norton.

————. 1990. "Only Man's Presence Can Save the Earth." Interview in *Harper's,* April.

Luke, Tim. 1987. "Deep Ecology and Distributive Justice." Paper presented at the Annual Meeting of the Midwest Political Science Association.

————. 1988. "The Dreams of Deep Ecology." *Telos,* no. 76 (Summer).

Macridis, Roy. 1992. *Contemporary Political Ideologies.* New York: HarperCollins.

Mandel, Tom. 1982. "Future Scenarios and Their Uses in Corporate Strategy." In *Business Strategy Handbook,* ed. Ken Albert. New York: McGraw-Hill.

Mandelbrot, Benoit. 1993. "Chaos Theory." Paper presented at the World Futures Studies Federation XIII World Conference, Turku, Finland, August 23.

Manes, Christopher. 1990a. *Green Rage.* Boston: Little, Brown.

————. 1990b. "Why I am a Misanthrope." *Earth First! Journal,* December 21.

Mannermaa, Mika. 1992. *Linking Present Decisions to Long-Range Visions.* Turku, Finland: The World Futures Studies Federation.

Marien, Michael. 1982. "The 'Transformation' As Sandbox Syndrome." *Association for Humanistic Pyschology Newsletter,* October.

Marks, Jodean. 1992. "Proposal for a Green Electoral Politics Conference." *The Greens Bulletin,* December.

Marx, Leo. 1964. *The Machine in the Garden: Technology and the Pastoral Ideal in America.* New York: Oxford University Press.

Maser, Chris. 1988. *The Redesigned Forest.* San Pedro: R. & E. Miles.

Masini, Eleonora. 1982. "Reconceptualizing Futures." *World Future Society Bulletin,* November/December.

McHale, John. 1969. *The Future of the Future.* New York: George Braziller.

McLaughlin, Corinne, and Gordon Davidson. 1986. *Builders of the Dawn.* Shutesbury, MA: Sirius.

Meeker-Lowrey, Susan. 1990. "Breaking Free: Building Bioregional Economies." In *Turtle Talk,* ed. Christopher Plant and Judith Plant. Philadelphia: New Society.

Merchant, Carolyn. 1980. *The Death of Nature: Women, Ecology and the Scientific Revolution.* San Francisco: Harper & Row.

————. 1990. "Ecofeminism and Feminist Theory." In *Reweaving the World,* ed. Irene Diamond and Gloria Feman Orenstein. San Francisco: Sierra Club Books.

Metzger, Deena. 1989. "Invoking the Grove." In *Healing the Wounds,* ed. Judith Plant. Philadelphia: New Society.

Mollison, Bill. 1988. *Permaculture: A Design Manual.* Tyalgum, NSW, Australia: Tagari Publications.

Muench, Mike. 1992. "Some Politics for a Green Party." *Green Synthesis*, no. 26 (August).

Muller-Rommel, Ferdinand. 1985. "The Greens in Western Europe." *International Political Science Review*. 6, no. 4.

Mumford, Lewis. 1966. *The Myth of the Machine*. New York: Harcourt Brace Jovaovich.

Mushaben, Joyce Marie. 1985-1986. "Innocence Lost." *New Political Science*, no. 14 (Winter).

Myers, Norman, ed. 1984. *Gaia: An Atlas of Earth Management*. Garden City, NY: Anchor Press/Doubleday.

Naess, Arne. 1973. "The Shallow and the Deep." *Inquiry*, no. 16.

———. 1988. "Identification as a Source of Deep Ecological Attitudes." In *Deep Ecology*, ed. Michael Tobias. San Marcos, CA: Avant Books.

Nanus, Burt. 1990. "Futures-Creative Leadership." *The Futurist* 24, no. 3 (May-June).

Nash, Roderick. 1988. "Rounding Out the American Revolution: Ethical Extension and the New Environmentalism." In *Deep Ecology*, ed. Michael Tobias. San Marcos, CA: Avant Books.

Newman, Steve. 1990. "Earthweek." *Sunday Star Bulletin and Advertiser* (Honolulu), September 16.

North American Bioregional Congress. 1987. *North American Bioregional Congress II Proceedings*. Forestville, CA: Hart.

Oates, David. 1989. *Earth Rising*. Corvallis, OR: Oregon State University Press.

O'Connor, Jennifer. 1989. "Ecology and Socialism." *The Activist*, no. 24 (March-April).

Ogden, Christopher. 1992. "No Third Parties Need Apply." *Time*, July 27.

Ogilvy, Jay. 1986. "The Current Shift of Paradigms." *ReVision* 9, no.1 (Summer/Fall).

Ogilvy, Jay, Eric Utne and Brad Edmondson. 1987. "Boom with a View." *Utne Reader*, no. 21 (May-June).

Orenstein, Gloria Feman. 1990. "Artists as Healers." In *Reweaving the World*, ed. Irene Diamond and Gloria Feman Orenstein, San Francisco: Sierra Club Books.

Ortega Gasset, Jose. 1985. *Meditations on Hunting*. New York: Scribner's.

Paige, Glenn D. 1977. *The Scientific Study of Political Leadership*. New York: Free Press.

———. 1980. "Non-violent Political Science." *Social Alternatives*, June.

———. 1983. "Nonviolence and Future Forms of Political Leadership." In *The Future of Politics*, ed. William Page. London: Frances Pinter.

———. 1992. "Introduction." In *Nonviolence Speaks to Power: Petra K. Kelly*. ed. Glenn D. Paige and Sarah Gilliatt. Honolulu: Center for Global Nonviolence Planning Project, Spark M. Matsunaga Institute for Peace.

———. 1993. *To Nonviolent Political Science*. Honolulu: Center for Global Nonviolence Planning Project, Spark M. Matsunaga Institute for Peace.

Papadakis, Elim. 1984. *The Green Movement in West Germany*. New York: St. Martin's Press.

Parkin, Sarah. 1989. *Green Parties: An International Guide*. London: Heretic Books.

Phillipose, Pamela. 1989. "Women Act: Women and Environmental Protection in India." In *Healing the Wounds*, ed. Judith Plant. Philadelphia: New Society.

Phillips, Kevin. 1990. *The Politics of Rich and Poor*. New York: Random House.

Pinchot, Gifford. 1947. *Breaking New Ground*. New York: Harcourt, Brace.

Plamenatz, John. 1970. *Ideology*. New York: Praeger.

"Planet Earth, How It Works, How To Fix It." 1988. *US News and World Report*, October 31.

"Planet of the Year." 1989. *Time*, January 2.

Plant, Christopher, and Judith Plant, eds. 1990. *Turtle Talk: Voices for a Sustainable Future*. Philadelphia: New Society.

———. 1991. *Green Business: Hope or Hoax?* Santa Cruz, CA: New Society.

Plant, Judith, ed. 1989. *Healing the Wounds: The Promise of Ecofeminism*. Philadelphia: New Society.

Poguntke, Thomas. 1993. *Alternative Politics—the German Green Party*. Edinburgh: Edinburgh University Press.

Pohl, Frederik. 1983. *Midas World*. New York: TOR.

Pohl, Frederik, and Lester del Rey. 1980. *Preferred Risk*. New York: Ballantine Books.

Pohl, Frederik, and C. M. Kornbluth. 1978. *The Space Merchants*. New York: Ballantine Books.

Porritt, Jonathon. 1985. *Seeing Green: The Politics of Ecology Explained*. Oxford: Basil Blackwell.

Postel, Sandra. 1990. "Saving Water for Agriculture." In *State of the World Atlas*, ed. Lester Brown. New York: Norton.

Rainbow, Stephen. 1993. "The New Zealand Values Party." In *Green Politics Two*, ed. Wolfgang Rudig. Edinbugh: Edinburgh University Press.

Register, Richard. 1987. *Ecocity Berkeley: Building Cities for a Healthy Future*. Berkeley, CA: North Atlantic Books.

Reich, Charles, A. 1970. *The Greening of America*. New York: Bantam Books.

Resenbrink, John. 1992. *The Greens and the Politics of Transformation*. San Pedro, CA: R & E Miles.

Rifkin, Carol. 1992. "The Greening of Capital Hill." *Utne Reader*, no. 53 (September-October).

Robbins, John. 1987. *Diet for a New America*. Walpole, NH: Stillpoint.

Rodman, John. 1983. "Defining an Environmental Ethic." In *Ethics and the Environment*, ed. Donald Scherer and Thomas Attig. Englewood Cliffs, NJ: Prentice Hall.

Rohter, Ira. 1992. *A Green Hawai'i: Sourcebook for Development Alternatives*. Honolulu: Na Kane O Ka Malo Press.

"The Role of Capitalism in Eco-Destruction Debated." 1989. *Green Tidings* 1, no. 2 (June 24).

Roselle, Mike. 1989. "Mike Roselle, Co-Founder of Earth First! on Direct Action." *Ecology Center Newsletter,* July.

Rothfeder, Jeffrey. 1989. "Is Nothing Private?" *Business Week*, September 4.

Rubenstein, Richard. 1970. *Rebels in Eden*. Boston: Little, Brown.

Rudig, Wolfgang, ed. 1991. *Green Party Members: A Profile*. Glasgow: Delta Publications.

———. 1993. *Green Politics Two*. Edinburgh: Edinburgh University Press.

Rudig, Wolfgang, and Mark Franklin. 1993. "Green Prospects: The Future of Green Parties in Britain, France and Germany." In *Green Politics Two*, ed. Wolfgang Rudig. Edinburgh: Edinburgh Univeristy Press.

Runte, Alfred. 1987. *National Parks, the American Experience*. Lincoln: University of Nebraska Press.

Russell, Julia Scofield. 1990. "Evolution of an Ecofeminist." In *Reweaving the World*, ed. Irene Diamond and Gloria Feman Orenstein. San Francisco: Sierra Club Books.

Russell, Peter. 1983. *The Global Brain*. Los Angeles: Tarcher.

Sale, Kirkpatrick. 1985. *Dwellers in the Land: The Bioregional Vision*. San Francisco: Sierra Club Books.

————. 1988. "Deep Ecology and Its Critics." *The Nation*, May 14.

————. 1990. "Foreword." In *Turtle Talk*, ed. Christopher Plant, and Judith Plant. Philadelphia: New Society.

Sargent, Lyman. 1988. *British and American Utopian Literature 1516-1974*. New York: Garland.

Sarkar, Saral. 1986. "The Green Movement in West Germany." *Alternatives*, April.

Satin, Mark. 1978. *New Age Politics: Healing Self and Society*. New York: Dell.

————. 1989. "Last Chance Saloon." *New Options*, June 30.

————. 1990a. "The 1980's were Better than We Thought." *New Options*, January-February.

————. 1990b. "You Don't Have To Be A Baby to Cry." *New Options*, September 24.

Scarce, Rik. 1990. *The Eco-Warriors*. Chicago: The Noble Press.

Schultz, Wendy. 1992. "Words, Dreams and Actions: Sharing the Futures Experience." In *Advancing Democracy and Participation: Challenged for the Future*, ed. B. Van Steenbergen, R. Nakarada, F. Marti, and J. Dator. Barcelona: Centre Catala de Prospectiva and Centre Unesco de Catalunya.

Schumacher, E.F. 1973. *Small is Beautiful: Economics as if People Mattered*. New York: Harper & Row.

Seed, John, Joanna Macy, Pat Fleming, and Arne Naess. 1988. *Thinking Like a Mountain: Towards a Council of All Beings*. Philadelphia: New Society.

Serpell, James. 1986. *In the Company of Animals*. New York: Basil Blackwell.

Setterberg, Fred. 1988. "The Wild Bunch: Earth First! Shakes Up the Environmental Movement." *Utne Reader*, May-June.

Seymour, Chris. 1992. "Third Party Organizing." *Z Magazine*, November.

Shannon, David. 1955. *The Socialist Party of America*. New York: Macmillan.

Shepard, Paul. 1973. *The Tender Carnivore and the Sacred Game*. New York: Scribner's.

Shepard, Paul and David McKinley, eds. 1969. *The Subversive Science*. Boston: HoughtonMifflin.

Simon, Julian, and Herman Kahn. 1984. *The Resourceful Earth*. New York: Basil Blackwell.

Singer, Peter. 1975. *Animal Liberation: A New Ethic for the Treatment of Animals*. New York: Avon Books.

Slaton, Christa Daryl. 1992. "The Failure of the United States Greens to Root in Fertile Soil." *Research in Social Movements, Conflicts and Change*, Supplement 2.

Slaughter, Richard. 1992. "Critical Future Studies and Worldview Design: Philosophical Issues in Future Studies." In *Advancing Democracy and Participation—Challenges for the Future*, ed. B. Van Steenbergen, R. Nakarada, F. Marti, and J. Dator. Barcelona: Centre Catala de Prospectiva and Centre Unesco de Catalunya.

Smith, Henry Nash. 1950. *Virgin Land*, New York: Vintage Books.

Snyder, Gary. 1985. "Four Changes." In *Deep Ecology*, ed. Bill Devall and George Sessions, Salt Lake City: Peregine Smith Books.

"SPAKA: Green Program USA." 1989. *Green Letter/Greener Times*. Special Edition (Autumn).

Spretnak, Charlene. 1978. Lost Goddesses of Ancient Greece. Berkeley: Moon Books.

————. 1981. *Lost Goddesses of Ancient Greece*. Boston: Beacon.

————, ed. 1982. *The Politics of Women's Spirituality*. New York: Anchor Books.

————. 1986. *The Spiritual Dimension of Green Politics*. Santa Fe: Bear.

————. 1989. "Toward an Ecofeminist Spirituality." In *Healing the Wounds*, ed. Judith Plant. Philadelphia: New Society.

————. 1990. "Ecofeminism: Our Roots and Flowering." In *Reweaving the World*, ed. Irene Diamond and Gloria Feman Orenstein. San Francisco: Sierra Club Books.

Starhawk. 1979. The Spiral Dance. San Francisco: Harper & Row.

————. 1982. "Consciousness, Politics and Magic." In *The Politics of Women's Spirituality*, ed. Charlene Spretnak. New York: Anchor Books.

————. 1987. *Truth or Dare: Encounters with Power, Authority and Mystery*. New York: Harper & Row.

————. 1989. "Feminist Earth-based Spirituality and Ecofeminism." In *Healing the Wounds*, ed. Judith Plant. Philadelphia: New Society.

————. 1990. "Power, Authority and Mystery: Ecofeminism and Earth-based Spirituality." In *Reweaving the World*, ed. Irene Diamond and Gloria Feman Orenstein. San Francisco: Sierra Club Books.

"Statement of the Strategic Policy Group on Lifeforms." 1989. *Green Letter/Greener Times*, Special Edition (Autumn).

Stone, Merlin. 1978. *When God was a Woman*. New York: Harcourt, Brace, Jovavich.

Swimme, Brian. 1986. "Paradigms and Paradigm Shifts." *Revision*, 9, no. 1.

————. 1990. "How to Heal a Lobotomy." In *Reweaving the World*, ed. Irene Diamond and Gloria Feman Orenstein. San Francisco: Sierra Club Books.

Talbot, Michael. *1986. Beyond the Quantum*. New York: Macmillan.

Teish, Luisah. 1985. *Jambalaya*. San Francisco: Harper & Row.

Thompson, William Irwin. 1985. *Pacific Shift*. San Francisco: Sierra Club Books.

————, ed. 1987. *Gaia: A Way of Knowing*. Great Barrington, MA: Lindesfarne Press.

Thoreau, Henry David. 1975. *The Selected Books of Thoreau*. Boston: HoughtonMifflin.

Thropy, Miss Ann. 1987. "Population and Aids." *Earth First! Journal*, May.

Tobias, Michael, ed. 1988. *Deep Ecology*. San Marcos, CA: Avant Books.

Todd, Nancy Jack and John Todd. 1984. *Bioshelters, Ocean Arks, City Farming: Ecology as the Basis of Design*. San Francisco: Sierra Club Books.

Toffler, Alvin. 1970. Future Shock. New York: Random House.

————. 1981. *The Third Wave*. New York: Bantam Books.

Tokar, Brian. 1987. *The Green Alternative*. San Pedro, CA: R & E Miles.

————. 1988. "Exploring the New Ecologies." *Alternatives*, 15, no. 4 (November-December).

————. 1989. "Ecological Radicalism." *Z Magazine*, February.

————. 1991. "The Greens: To Party or Not?" *Z Magazine*, October.

Toulmin, Stephen. 1982. *The Return to Cosmology*. Berkeley: University of California Press.

Toynbee, Arnold. 1972. *A Study of History*. Oxford: Oxford University Press.

————. 1976. *Mankind and Mother Earth: A Narrative History of the World*. New York: Oxford University Press.

Trachtenberg, Alan. 1982. *The Incorporation of America*. New York: Hill & Wang.

Van Steenbergen, B., R. Nakarada, F. Marti, and J. Dator, eds. 1992. *Advancing Democracy and Participation—Challenges for the Future*. Barcelona: Centre Catala de Prospectiva and Centre Unesco de Catalunya.

Valaskakis, Kimon, ed. 1979. *The Conserver Society: A Workable Alternative for the Future*. New York: Harper & Row.

Vishvanatha (Bob Kaplan). 1988. "Morality and Social Progress." *Pasaka'*, January.

"Waif at the Heart of a Revolution." 1983. *London Times Magazine*. February 28.

Walker, Timothy. 1831. "Defence of Mechanical Philosophy." *North American Review*, no. 33 (July).

Walljasper, Jay. 1987. "The Prospects for Green Politics in the U.S." *Utne Reader*, September/October.

———. 1989. "Can Green Politics Take Root in the US?" *Utne Reader*, September/October.

Warner, Marina. 1976. *Alone of All Her Sex*. New York: Knopf.

Warren, Karen. 1987. "Feminism and Ecology." *Environmental Ethics*, no. 1.

Warren, Peter. 1984. "Knossos." *Archaeology*, July-August.

Wattenberg, Ben. 1985. *The Good News Is, The Bad News Is Wrong*. New York: Simon & Schuster.

Webster, Daniel. [1903] 1964. "Opening of the Northern Railroad." In *The Writings and Speeches of Daniel Webster*. As cited in Leo Marx, *The Machine in the Garden*. Oxford: Oxford University Press.

Wiesenthal, Helmut. 1993. *Realism in Green Politics*, ed. John Ferris. Manchester: Manchester University Press.

Williams, R. 1977. *Marxism and Literature*. Oxford: Oxford University Press.

Williams, Samuel. [1809] 1983. *The Natural and Civil History of Vermont*. As cited in William Cronon, *Changes in the Land*. New York: Hill & Wang.

Wilson, Ian. 1978. "Scenarios." In *The Procedures of Futures Research*, ed. Jib Fowles, Westport, CT: Greenwood Press.

Wilson, Marie. 1989. "Wings of the Eagle." In Healing the Wounds, ed. Judith Plant. Philadelphia: New Society.

Woodcock, George. 1990. "Mutual Aid." In *Turtle Talk*, ed. Christopher Plant and Judith Plant, Philadelphia: New Society.

Wyatt, Mike. 1989. "Humanism and Ecology." *Green Synthesis*, issue 32 (October).

Zimmerman, Michael. 1990. "Deep Ecology and Ecofeminism: The Emerging Dialogue." In *Reweaving the World*, ed. Irene Diamond and Gloria Feman Orenstein. San Francisco: Sierra Club Books.

Zuckerman, Seth. 1987. "A Grassroots Rebellion Revamps Environmentalism." *Utne Reader*, no. 21 (May/June).

Index

About the Author

KENN KASSMAN holds a Ph.D. from the University of Hawaii and has taught at the Technical University of Berlin, Schiller International University, also in Berlin, and the University of Hawaii.

ISBN 0-275-95784-5

90000>

EAN

9 780275 957841

HARDCOVER BAR CODE